My Higher Kingdom

Men, May I Seduce You?

Ladies, please join me.

Heart, Mind & Body Wellness

By

Andrea Elliott

Hello Brave Reader,

Welcome to a taste of inspiration. Thank you for purchasing my book! Although you probably have not met anyone quite like me, that doesn't mean we aren't more alike than different. What's important to note is that I express my heart and truth without apology.

My intellectual mind, affectionate heart and aware body has a vested interest in the new human we are becoming. My voice is here to inform, connect and transform. You are the one who guides you.

I subscribe to the values of truth, clarity and connection. It is from that place that I reach out to you with my sensual nature to invite more of who you are - to the table of life. The platter of power I summon is no joke. That doesn't mean we can't have fun.

My personal insights from overcoming loss, facing challenges, and diving under the covers with diverse and interesting men from all walks of life, have brought me deeper understandings of my limitless nature beyond the programs of the past. The light I shed will help you to see more too.

Names of the men in this book are a product of my imagination. The places, adventures, loves and losses are my real-life experiences.

Let the wings of the back cover inspire your own to rise up and expand out!

The information provided in this book are my perspectives and experiences and are not intended as a substitute for the medical advice of physicians. If you wish to apply ideas contained in this book, you are taking full responsibility for your actions. My goal is to share my freedom for you to claim more of your own. Now let's take flight together.

Warmly,
Andrea

2

Art & Design

Wings by Melanie Ann Lambert Art. They sprung from the back of my book ~ thanks to the love of Dennis Owens and the beautiful cover he designed for me.

ISBN: 978-1-7352257-0-8 Paperback

ISBN: 978-1-7352257-2-2 eBook

3

Table of Contents

Introduction

The Striptease:

In becoming a wildly alive human in female form, I had to step off of the carpet ride of shame and guilt. Whether you are a man or a woman, I guarantee you have known repression. To discover my own true nature, I had to gain sight of old programs and patterns. Let me share with you what I learned about the process of stripping and how alive I feel in my naked freedom because I'd like you to join me. If you wish.

I was once mired in limited beliefs, societal conditioning, and bad habits that prevented me from seeing just how strapped down and gagged I was, until I ripped free. That was where everything real became unreal, and all that was unreal became real. It was a big change, similar to the start of 2020 and how life is no longer the same. The death of the old me was like dying to the shell of the person that was me.

An outer authority had designed the old version of me and those programs ran inside my mind. Limited thinking was the only reality I knew, until I asked, "Who am I?" And "Why am I here?" The answers came by discovering who I was not, or what was not true.

Now stripped of the old, I am naked in my true self, here to seduce you with my playful, wide-open heart and sensual nature. The authentic me, found underneath the filth of shame, guilt, and unworthiness programs is now sparkling and shining a starlight of inspiration, that's reaching out to you. I'm here to ask you to join me in becoming your highest and greatest potential.

Facing societal, familial, and governmental programming, along with religious dogma that defined my former existence wasn't easy but I'm going to challenge you to do the same - in your own way. I'm inviting you to get naked (vulnerable and real) with me. I want you to get honest with yourself, right here and right now. And that will require some stripping. **I would like to help you undress** because I'd like you to join me. I need you and I'll tell you why.

I Need You.

I welcome your participation and consideration in addressing an urgent and massive problem we all are facing. The current definition of success, and the foundation of business and government is void of heart. Those who have been in control of what we were told to believe, steered us away from knowing who we are in: mind, heart and body. That's not something we can shrug off any longer because there's more for us to realize and bring forth in our human potential. It may not seem obvious to you in this moment, to the extent you have bought into the program of limitation, or how you may be perpetuating a cycle that's come to its end. I need you to stick with me because you are involved and there's more for you to know.

Dehumanization, disconnection, and desensitizing people through war, violence, abuse of power, stress, mainstream media, movies, television, video games, drugs, porn, alcohol and the act of keeping us busy, rushing and "doing" is now up for change.

Please don't walk away and think this has nothing to do with you, because it does. It will affect you and your business in the years to come. You want to stick around and listen to what I have to share. Even if it seems a little uncomfortable or when you think it doesn't relate to you… because it does.

It's time to make a choice. We are all responsible for our participation, even if we don't choose to participate. That is also a choice. We must see where the character traits and situations in our own business and personal lives are abusive and unacceptable, in order to become the solution. We don't have the luxury of ignoring this any longer. There's a new creation at hand.

Change is here, and it's here to stay. I'm going to help you understand the significance of this change and how to get comfortable with the discomfort because we've got to bring ourselves online. There may be a vast separation that occurs between those who participate and those who do not. Two very different worlds may take form. I'm speaking to those who would like to participate in this massive and important change in human history, by tapping into their highest and greatest potential. Are you curious about your limitless nature?

The lack of heart in the form of abuse of power, has hit center stage, as men in executive and political positions have gone from hero to zero in a snap. That will continue. Many leaders and CEOs have stepped down (behind the scenes) in the last two years. We will continue to see the demolition of the old reality and the removal of big players as **power is redefined**. You will want to keep reading to see how you are involved and what practical steps you can take in your own lives, to be a part of the solution.

The way business, media, society, some religion, and our government have operated in the past, stepped on the hearts of humanity. Shaming and controlling people's beliefs, feelings, thoughts, bodies and habits; to fit a narrative of limitation, disconnection and dehumanization. You may not realize just yet, how you came to accept the normal that is now changing.

I fell into the trap myself, but began waking up many years ago to the psychological manipulation of my own consciousness. That has made most people unaware that they are being enslaved. Many have no clue that they are deprived of knowledge, made to believe emotions and their bodies are unsafe. They are being held in a frequency of limitation. When you get out of that prison of ignorance - you will come to see exactly what I mean.

In the months and years to come, we will see the old structures continue to fall away. My request of asking if I may seduce you is about inspiring you to choose a higher kingdom within yourself, to fill the void of the old that's clearing out. That kingdom is your Infinite Spirit or Highest Self. Life is not going back to the way it was because something brand new is taking form.

I am here to inform, teach from experience, inspire and evolve with you, as we go through this process of purification and empowerment together. I will give you a variety of perspectives to inspire higher states of consciousness and offer practical steps that aided my process of change. I will be throwing out ideas and analogies for your consideration. And sharing personal experiences and choices that I made that can bring awareness to your thoughts and ideas.

Why do you want to listen to me? Because my heart cares about humanity and this important opportunity that's before us. My purpose in life is to assist others in times of great change. I'm a Teacher who empowers and inspires others to put words to their own feelings and personal experiences by sharing mine - to spark their awareness. My affectionate heart cares deeply and is here to serve a significant role at this time.

I am an expert in the field of transformation and personally know what that means and what it entails. That change will look different for each of you. I understand the massive opportunity and the work that is here before us, and would like to clarify the process for your consideration. This work I'm speaking about is an inside job, and it requires an independent responsibility. A decision and contribution that affects every single person... starting with you. As a playful, caring, sensual, intelligent and inspiring woman, I promise to command the very best in you. If you would like the push - the coach in me will give it to you.

The change I am speaking about requires your consent and daily commitment. It's a personal process of becoming the new model of man. That will feel uncomfortable at times. It will challenge you and it will ultimately transform you, and all of mankind. It is a process that will take us from ordinary to extraordinary so expect to sweat.

The value of human existence is what is at hand. It's that big of a deal. And I am a forerunner who expects to inspire a kingdom of lions to their greatness. I affectionally refer to the men who read this book as my lions. My Inner Spark is motivating yours to ignite and light your own way. My words are here to inform, inspire and cuddle you along the way. When you need more than a cuddle, the lion tamer in me can command more.

If you let me sensually love you through these pages, while you push ahead in the direction that's right for you, we can rise up together. I trust that along the way, you will shed the lower dimensions of limitations, and allow your physical body to hold a higher frequency - to go from ordinary to extraordinary.

This ride we are going on will take you from a belief in limitation, to the highway of infinite possibilities. It will require you stepping into your high-performance vehicle. To gain access to that highway you will be engaging with the things that frighten you. When you do… nothing can control you. Then the open highway will be all yours.

I'm here to support that change. I am here to inform you of what that may look like, how change impacted me, and what practical steps you can take to support your body, heart and mind. The sweet icing on top of this multidimensional cake is your own freedom.

Along the way, you may imagine me sensually whispering in your ear, "You can do this!" Because I understand change can be tough. I know what it takes to engage with the things that frighten us. This book is written for those who accept the challenge of redefining success, power and leadership in our world today- by transforming you from the inside out.

We Are the Result of Our Thoughts:

Those who have been in charge never wanted us to know about our limitless nature, and that we are here to evolve. They didn't want us to discover the power of our hearts and the wisdom in our bodies. Or about natural law because their fear tactics and mind control would no longer have power over us. They wanted to keep us in the dark, which is where lack of information exists. I'm here to wake you up.

If you knew from the start that you were the results of your thoughts, would you have chosen to think differently? Our thoughts are either empowering or disempowering. Did you know that most people don't think for themselves and don't even know it? How do I know this? Because I was one of them; a person living off of programs installed at birth and reinforced through daily conditioning. Many people are also disconnected from their feelings or emotional body. I was one of those people too.

Today, I am free. I made it here without many role models to lead the way. It was a messy process going from being told who I was, to discovering who I was not. Every crisis, challenge and new experience brought me learning opportunities. You can read about some of my intimate experiences in Part II. That section is designed for the ladies. However, it may be tempting for the men to read as well.

In short, it's now time for each of us to raise our standards. For me, it was a choice to become my highest and greatest potential. That required gaining sight of habits, beliefs and character traits that were in the way of my greatness. By making the choice to rise up; you will also have the opportunity to discover what is keeping you from being all you are capable of being.

If you are interested in becoming a free agent, knowing what it means to be sovereign, awake and aware in the world today – then step right up. That choice means you let go of the herd and give up your sheep status, and be willing to be challenged like never before. This opportunity is for the strong at heart to become the new model of man. Please keep reading because I want you!

I am calling the most courageous leaders of our time. I need you men, and you know who you are. Feel my words and let them carry you with me. I am affectionately respecting you every step of the way. Even when things don't make sense, I am believing in you.

The work I am inspiring you to do isn't something anyone can do for you. It's an inside job and it requires your daily commitment. I know the strength and power of personal development. It's why I'm here cheering you on. This isn't about a physical relationship with me, let me make that clear. One day you may meet me in person, and perhaps work with me one-on-one. But this is all about you. And an important transition that many of us will continue to go through - in discovering our sense of Self in every moment.

I believe in each and every one of you, and I am here on behalf of becoming my highest and greatest potential. My investment is my limitless nature and the greater good of all. It's from that place I am inviting you to join me, in remembering your Infinite Spirit. When you go into this process with awareness you can better navigate your way by listening to your body. This is about more of who you are. You'll need your heart and body as your guide - not just your mind.

What You Can Expect:

To be inspired! I also offer insight on possible blind spots and encourage changes that make room for your heart to feel again. Don't get stuck on any one idea. But rather notice where you are resistant, fearful or hesitant. When you observe those parts of yourself you create an opportunity for liberation. In other words, you go from the slow lane of limitation, into the highway of information - from dark to light.

Letting in new information is allowing in new possibilities. No matter what situation you find yourself in, it is the power of your thoughts that got you there. Your perceptions control your behavior. Let's see if we can broaden them.

What many people don't realize is that there is no greater power than what's in the heart. If you don't believe me, you'll discover the truth of what I am saying when you experience a closer relationship with your body. If you stick with me through these pages I am confident you will gain sight of what is in the way of gaining more of your power.

Even Einstein was too afraid to share what he knew about the power of the heart while he was alive. He left the knowledge in a letter to his daughter and he asked her to release the information when society was ready to know that his research concluded something far greater than his theory of relativity. Read some of Einstein's words from his personal letter to his daughter below:

"There is an extremely powerful force that scientists have not yet found a formal explanation to. It is a force that includes and governs all others. This universal force is love. It is the most powerful unseen force. Love is light that enlightens those who give and receive it. Love is power because it multiplies the best we have and allows humanity not to be extinguished in their blind selfishness. This force explains everything and gives meaning to life. This is the variable we have avoided far too long. It's the only energy in the universe that man has not learned to drive at will.

If instead of E=MC2, we accept that the energy to heal the world can be obtained through love multiplied by the speed of light squared. We conclude that love is the most powerful force there is because it has no limits. If we want our species to survive, if we are to find meaning in life and want to save every sentient being in the world, love is the only answer." Referenced from www.thejourney.com.

If you don't believe Einstein's findings, I trust you believe in you. And that is why you have become a part of an army of men who will rise to a new level of success, and become the new standard of what it means to be a man in the world today. I'm asking you to join me in being a part of the solution, and in what will be a revolution. The greatest story in history is right now in the making. It's the new model of human we are now becoming.

Get Naked with Me.

I am inviting you to slip under the covers with me. Just you and me. We'll do this together. To be clear, I'm not trying to take you away from a relationship. I'm offering my playful, inspiring nature to affectionately support the most important relationship in your life. The relationship with your Higher Self. When you align with your inner guidance, you will move mountains by living with purpose. You will receive the reassurance of what comes next, each time you reconcile what has come before.

This is a process, and it is why I have put my tingling, vivacious vibrations into each and every word in this book. When you are feeling challenged by life or my perspectives and daily exercises, please sense that I am still affectionately respecting you. I'm holding you close to me and seeing the very best in you… every step of the way. You are a good man, whose heart matters and our world needs. Please keep me in your imagination and stick with me through these pages.

I love that sharp mind of yours, and I would like to help you mine the gold in your heart so we can see what is hidden inside. I'm going to inspire you to take back more of your own power and to move to a new level of performance. I've simplified ideas in this book for the smartest of men, whether spiritual, emotional or not.

Ladies,

I invite you to join me to see what I have learned in becoming awake and aware in body, mind and heart. Part II is all for you. Beyond raising the bar for these great men, I share sexual experiences that helped me move beyond body and sexual shame for you to see what I learned. By the touch of my skin, I slowly shed the old programs and came to discover my body and its pleasure - as sacred and wise.

My experiences also brought about a unique touch that men really love. I can inform you about this on a phone or video call session, for you to try on your partner. The men who have been on the receiving end of my touch, in my personal relationships, insist others need to know that men love to be touched this way. Although I do share knowledge that I have gained, this specific piece wasn't something I was going to include in my book. The men in my life were adamant that I use my voice to inform others so that more men can receive this in their relationships. I'm sure women will like it as much as men do.

In the heart of compassion, and in the belief of our human potential - we learn and grow together. When we support each other we bring about new possibilities. I hope that each of you feel inspired to write to me, to share what you have learned about yourself and what it means to heal and evolve in our world today. Enjoy what I share with you in Part II about healing my body, mind and heart.

Ladies & Gentlemen,

If you are currently unaware of what it means to become en**light**ened, I'm glad you found this book. Although, it is a very individual process and unfolds in each step that you take, it's already your state of being. It's time to notice the "light" in the center of who you are. If we spoke in frequency terms you would understand it is about raising your frequency. The light in you is turning up in volume. Since you can't physically see your light, I am directing you to tune into your vibe. I'm teaching you about sensing your heart. That is what will help you to gain clarity about the direction you choose to take at this time.

Personally, I'm still reaping the dividends from my choice. However, it did come at a price. Letting go of what no longer served me. I'm in still in that practice of letting go of old programs because I'm all about downloading the newest upgrades in my operating system. The most important technology I possess is within me. If you would like to be on the cutting edge of the human potential - join in. It's important to realize that we are the most advanced technology in the years to come. I'll talk about turning on my technology as the scientist

18

and researcher of my own limitless potential. And why I'm seducing you to do the same.

I'm not here to battle you or to defend my perceptions but I am here to open you up to new possibilities. I dare to explore my limitless nature and to follow my own internal guidance. There's no finish line, it's an ongoing process. My experiences and understanding may inspire new thoughts about life and love and encourage a closer relationship with your Higher Self. This isn't about me being any better than you, this is about me sharing my freedom with you.

The important thing for us all to remember, is that we must learn to ride the wave of change because it is our new normal. We can continue to see new possibilities as we realize more of our highest and greatest potential. Getting to know our heart is essential. It communicates to us through our body because the physical is the spiritual. You do not need to use the word spiritual but you do need to be in touch with your body. Our heart speaks through our physical form. Since these times are about change and choice; how are you going to ride the wave of change in your life? Any good surfer knows - the only way to ride a wave is with balance.

In my classroom and gym, you will learn that balance includes: mental, physical, emotional, and spiritual well-being. What I see happening at this time in history is the collapse of a patriarchal society, steeped in limitation and control, and the rising up of our limitless potential. As we do this together - we write the greatest story in history. Call it whatever you like, but do take an independent responsibility in your own personal development as your contribution to the whole. It's your choice and no one can make it but **you**.

Invest in Your Unused Potential:

Most people are operating through repetitive habits, and are using 10% or less of their conscious mind per Dr. Bruce Lipton, developmental biologist. They have been trapped in the frequency of limitation, in my words. I was once one of those people, and now I'm upping the game baby because I want us to rise together! That's right. I am going to offer you exercises, perspectives and new ideas, to inspire your unused potential. I was able to tap into more, and so can you!

We house a complex operating system within us but only we can turn it on and tap into the quantum field of infinite possibilities within us. No one can do it for us. This book will give you the practical steps I used to support my process, which can help you strengthen and flex your muscle of awareness.

My unique life experience and the things I discovered may help you strip a little easier. This book encourages you to see old habits, to reconnect with your heart, and to integrate a new level of success as a man in the world today. With a balance of mind and heart, I automatically brought more of my Spirit into my physical form.

The 90% of our unused potential isn't found in the things we are habitually doing. It's found in the places we've been ignoring, avoiding, resisting, denying, shaming and not willing to open to.

That is why I will make you sweat or perhaps turn away at times, but I trust you will stay in the game. Consider me a personal trainer and coach who is challenging you to transform more than just your body. Can we stretch your mind and expand your heart too?

I will teach and challenge you to respect aspects of yourself seen as weaknesses, flaws, or defects and I will encourage you to face fears and let go of old habits that have kept you stuck and unchangeable. We were born as unique individuals for a reason. All of our differences are gifts to one another. Let me help you to see more of what makes you special.

My perspectives will challenge the "man box" rules you've been living by because life taught us to eliminate, deny or destroy natural aspects of who we are by portraying them as weak. To learn how to feel again; begin by giving yourself space to notice when you block these aspects. Your muscle of awareness grows bigger as you gain sight of habits that are ready to fall away. What potential are you blocking?

The ladies will be challenged in their own way throughout Part II. It's an opportunity to observe the relationship with your own body. Gaining sight of any disconnect is an area of unused potential that resides in your biology.

For the men and women who stick around to the very end, you will find my contact information if you would like to talk with me via phone, email or in person. I welcome the opportunity to hear from you and would love to know what you received from this book.

Men, if you have been trained to remain silent, to play tough, to hide your feelings, and to fit-in; I'm going to challenge you to bust out, break free and rise up with me. I am going to joyfully blow your mind and strip you naked, and inspire you to open up to what lies within your heart as your infinite potential. You are now in my territory where a depth of courage, feminine sensuality and personal mastery exists. Welcome to my world.

Are You Ready to Go Inside?

Gentlemen, I would now like to lead you inward but to see into that dark void you must gain skills that require you to sense and feel again. Those skills are more natural than you realize. What I am here to remind you is - there is much more to life and to who you are, then what your eyes can see. May I lube you up and guide you in slowly and deeply… into more of who you are? If the answer is yes, I am reaching out to guide you in.

PART I: Busting Out

Welcome to a time of great change! This is my area of expertise as a woman of transformation, I am well equipped for these times. If you don't know what is going on yet, I will open your eyes to the realization that we are in the experience of incorporating more of our Infinite Spirit. I do use Infinite Spirit, Inner Spark, Source and Higher Self interchangeably. Whatever word you like to use to represent what lies in your heart - is up to you.

The realization of who we are is a process, that is now happening at a rapid pace. Nothing will be the same again because change is here to stay. That leaves a lot of room for uncertainty. That is scary for most people but I am not like most people. I withdrew my consent to the former reality and my life is no longer as I once knew it. I understand how this works and I can help you broaden your understanding too. Consider me your resource if any of these ideas are new to you.

I stand as one of many conscious humans who are tapping into their limitless nature. Life is being redefined and we have no idea how that will impact each person who opens to their highest and greatest potential. We get to feel, sense and live in the Infinite, more each day. This quantum field is within you too.

When you choose to become more aware of this process, you will observe more of your human potential by developing a relationship with your Higher Self. New data in the form of information is available just like software upgrades. We get to watch the old data departing and make room for our new upgrade to take form. We do that by identifying or observing the things in our life that must go. In my life, those are old habits and beliefs that have become patterns. When I asked, "Who am I?" I got to see who I was not but who I actually thought I was. Each time I saw aspects of my beliefs that defined me, they had less of a control over me.

When the old clutter was removed, the higher intelligence that resides in my heart expanded into the new space provided. The new habits I formed helped me to strengthen the connection to my higher intelligence. Alignment was key to me maintaining my high-performance vehicle, which had more precision capabilities than my former make and model.

I went through similar transitions in shedding the old. Each time it required me to take the step of reconciliation or self-forgiveness to heal and let go of the past, old clutter. Just like getting my body into shape, there were daily practices (that I still do today) that supported my transition and helped me maintain my focus and discipline.

One of the most important qualities you already possess, if you have known success in business or in raising a family, is the ability to take responsibility. That is an important quality that will come in handy with the task at hand.

Consider these ideas below as takeaways:

- Change is normal, necessary, and transformative. By letting go of the old (limitations) we make room for the new (information).
- Disconnect and separation causes suffering and is being replaced with connection to heart and others.
- Different is not bad. It can be transformational.
- Men have permission to feel again.
- It's natural and important to ask for consent and help.
- Merging feeling (feminine) and logic (masculine) is a natural step in our evolution.
- Building our muscle of awareness supports our mind, heart and body wellness.

Pep Talk:

I am here to encourage you to become the best man you can be. This requires bravery and an independent responsibility from each and every one of you. I know what it takes because I've been in the practice of: living by choice, co-creating with the universe, and becoming more conscious each day. It hurt like hell at times when my muscle of awareness exposed aspects of me that weren't easy to see, or lies that I believed were truth. But I know you can do this. I believe in you!

Going from the mindset of limitation and victimhood, where others have told you what to think and believe, to being a creator of your own reality through choice, is a significant and extraordinary shift. We are changing so quickly now that you will want to keep an eye out for my next book as this one will run its course as we upgrade. That is because the new model of man is on the rise.

Discovering my sense of Self in every moment is a freedom I have come to experience as my "new normal." It's exciting and new as my mind continues to expand with my heart's potential. That doesn't mean I don't experience difficulty. I just navigate with more tools. It's very much like becoming the CEO of your life but larger in the experience because it's a power that is alive within you. Life becomes richer in ways you never imagined, when you align with your Higher Self. Quite simply, we are on a journey of awakening to our greatest potential.

It is with deep respect that I am here in full participation in support of this change and transformation. My sensual, sassy and playful nature is cheering this movement onward and upward. Consider this book my legacy of love as I choose to inspire you to reach for your highest and greatest potential to rise with me.

I remember what it was like to learn to open my heart. It wasn't easy at first but it was worth every effort because of the results. Today, I live in a success steeped in peace that others recognize and sense. This wealth is within me. As is my power of love that lives in every breath that I take, and weaves its power in all that I create. My heart brings me deep satisfaction and is fueled by the way that I care for it. A healthy diet of play and wonder are a must. I enjoy and appreciate unimaginable opportunities, and endless present moment experiences that tickle my heart playful. I am living my life purpose, enjoying every dynamic, considerate and generous person that enters my life as a client, friend or associate.

Earlier in life, I thought I had it all and I didn't possess most of the things I just mentioned. In other words, you don't know what you are missing - until you know it exists. I would like to give you a taste of what I know is possible, but it's going to cost you the things that need to fall away.

I'm excited for those of you who want to see your strength of heart play out in the game of life. It's okay to find yourself anxious and uncertain at times as you do this. But those aren't reasons to stop you. There is pain to be felt but it doesn't last forever. Remember, I'm looking for the very best in you and I do expect to see you sweat. However, it is you who remains in charge of this inside job. The energy of "busting out" is already here and will continue to blow open the lives of many. You can resist it and make things more difficult for yourself. You can also choose to become more informed to support your own process of change.

None the less, your perspiration may have already begun and could intensify when you realize that life and business needs you to slow down your thinking. It's a special skillset to learn to listen to the silence. The wise man in you knows that the silence has something important to teach you. This request to slow down is both a warning and an opportunity. We are in the midst of an expansion hence the "busting out" of the old.

Your heart has been communicating to you. You've been in the habit of avoiding and denying what it has to say and now you have me to deal with me. Giggle, giggle. I am here to give the heart a voice so that you can hear it more clearly because it's ready to expand in you.

I'm not speaking to those who cower to conformity in complete resistance to the change at hand. I understand that some people will go the opposite direction and not even realize it. For those of you who are willing to broaden your perspective, and for those who may need a little extra gentle smack on the bum (metaphorically speaking) to wake you up from your submission, I'm here to do just that.

I am calling the strong-minded leaders who challenge their thoughts and dare to take an honest look at themselves. Those of you who are more motivated by a caring, sensual, smarty pants like me, who can challenge your intellect and motor your heart – here I am! I will wave the flag at the starting line of your highest and greatest potential and say, "Fire up your engines boys! It's time to bust out of the slow lane and head onto the highway of infinite intelligence within you!" I want to see what you got. The seen and the unseen is what I'll bring to you.

Chapter 1
Who Are You?

Let me answer that first by introducing myself. My name is Andrea. I am a wildly alive, petite brunette with dark brown eyes, a warm smile and an affectionate heart. I want to pull you in and snuggle you up... into your greatness. You have my permission to imagine my outer beauty however you wish because it is my inner kingdom where I invite you to come. And I inspire you to erect it within yourself too.

I am an Inspirational Teacher and a dynamic coach, who works with the entire scope of what makes us human. The mind, body, and heart are all on board when I enter the room. I notice some of you smart and handsome men are arriving in my classroom intellectually superior. I don't mind that at all. I like powerful and smart men. Perhaps a warning though - some of my perspectives, exercises and ideas may push up against your strong minds. They may seem far too simple but don't let that stop you. If you stick with me, you will reach a higher standard of performance and have fun along the way.

Who knows, maybe you'll even meet me in person by signing up for my six-pack session to discover more of who you are. It's important to note that I don't work with everyone in the same way. Each person is at a very different place of learning. Over six sessions, you will come to see how intimate you are with your own heart, mind and body. It's a self-discovery process and no two people are alike. It is fun to get to know yourself on a deeper level. When you do that with someone who is open to their authentic self you automatically access more of the same in you. My freedom is inspiring - beware.

In addition to phone sessions, where people gain clarity, insights, receive supportive listening, and unload worries, I do meet in person with clientele of my choosing. I value my time and the quality of people I choose to work with in person, and that requires knowing more about you first. My clients are loyal, considerate, intelligent and kind people. I work with a diverse, ever-growing clientele. I am not a licensed therapist or counselor. I am woman who will inspire and inform you in ways that are unique to you.

Thanks to my clients pushing me to offer myself to others, I have published this book to reach out to you - wherever you are in the world. If my inspiration and insights rub you just the right way, you can learn how to contact me at the end of this book. For now, our work together begins right here. In the future, I will have a school to serve other generations in a group setting.

This book is about knowing thyself. When I ask you, "Who are you?" You must remember your heart in order to truly answer that question. The personal work I am teaching will make space for your heart to be heard to guide you. The heart has a very clear purpose. I am here in support of its remembrance.

The power of the heart had been forgotten. It is now safe for it to be remembered. From the moment it is developed, it beats to keep us alive. I'm taking you back to the womb where your life started and your first organ formed in our body. Your heart gave you life. Other natural components of our formation were - surrender and trust. We were vulnerable, innocent, and pure and had no desire to harm ourself or our mother. We also had the natural ability to sense. Our extrasensory perception was our only form of communication. All of this important machinery is wired into us. These qualities are the foundation of who we are in our purest form. Parts of this operating system have been forgotten or turned off. It's time to get them back online.

Lucky for me, fear and resistance to these natural parts of who we are have not stopped me from learning to accept them within me. If they weren't treasures worth remembering, I wouldn't waste your time returning you to the womb. Back to the brick and mortar of who you are to bring them back online.

My expertise in the unseen realms, allows me to be a lion tamer of sorts as I work with strong-minded men who have established habits of denying their feelings and using logic alone. When I say strong-minded, I mean intelligent men with well-developed minds. If you are one of those men, allow me to begin massaging you to open you up to something more. And realize, I'm not really taming you but rather inspiring the real wildness, only found in the heart, to be set free.

The power and speed of your high-performance vehicle is based on the weight of your engine/heart. Seeing the things that weigh it down is important to gain sight of. If you want to open to the highway of your greatest potential you need to clean out those valves, by getting honest with yourself.

No man needs to take from a woman to remember what's already inside of him. The priceless components of your operating system have not left you. Your heart is valuable. It's needed and its appreciated. Your mind is exquisite. And your body – well? You tell me. How are you caring for it?

Most people do not get the opportunity to see the full scope of who they are because they let life sidetrack them. They were told what to believe and they anchored that limited thinking into their life through patterns and habits. They thought life was based on their bank accounts, their status, material possessions, business connections, or intellectual IQ.

Many don't even see their arrogance, condescension, or selfish nature because life rewarded them for caring only about themselves, their families, what they accumulated, leveraged, schemed, manipulated, or built for themselves. They live in the model of 'service to self' and are blind to their habitual behaviors and ignorance. Many don't realize that each of us is responsible for perpetuating limitation, until we see where those character traits exist in us or in our immediate environment.

Living a life where the mind wins and the body and heart have little room to be seen, appreciated, and valued is - not living. It's surviving. This is a problem and it can only be solved by each person taking an independent responsibility to become more aware of who they are and who they are not.

You do not get entry into my classroom based on your intellect alone or your title, but your willingness to take responsibility for your life, along with your desire to participate in this great change does. This first section is not only for successful men to enter, it's for all who are willing to learn and grow. With the exception of socio-paths, narcissists or beings void of Source connection. I just want to make that clear. I do not extend my energy in their direction.

Those of you who are with me, let your senses come alive as you read. I would like to be a supportive force in your life. The great men that I work with daily enrich my life. If you would, please consider yourself a new man in my life who is important to me. If you are a woman reading this section, you matter to me. I continue to help women through similar challenges that I have faced and overcome. The start of Part II will clue you in on those similarities. Taking care of each other is what love is for. Our care must begin with the relationship with ourself first.

I welcome all of you into the kingdom of your Infinite Spirit. I believe there's no greater place to reside and it's why I call my book and my podcast, My Higher Kingdom. I am living heaven on earth through the heart of who I am. Thank you for investing in you, and for supporting my work in the world by purchasing this book. I respect and appreciate each and every one of you. May my mind and heart inspire you to know more of who you are.

Chapter 2
Welcome to My Classroom & Gym

Class has begun. Up until now, the definition of success has not included heart. The men who are reading this book are being asked to raise their standards. Business and life in general are beckoning the whole of the human beyond just the mind. Logic and reason only - does not make room for heart. That's a habit that must change. I'm sure many of you want to defend both logic and reason but please remain open and stick with me please. We can't grow our businesses of tomorrow or ourselves, without bringing more heart into the equation.

Let me break this down for you. We have a body that requires maintenance and self-care. It is the vessel that holds the mind and heart. The physical is the spiritual and it communicates with our heart through our body. The heart is the activity of feeling and uses intuition or gut instincts to arrive at insights. That is why it's important to become cognizant of the heart through your body signals. It is how we discern the guidance of our Infinite Spirit or Higher Self. This is by no means a religion. These are simply aspects of our human existence. And it's time to wake-up to them.

Why would we leave these valuable parts of who we are out of our business or personal lives? Not acknowledging or providing for our heart and body is living life from the shoulders up. It's how we remained limited. Can you imagine getting into your car and being unaware that the four tires require balancing and that the engine needs regular maintenance? The parts of us that keep us in the present moment are meant to be acknowledged. Not just the ignition that turns the mind of the car on.

Think about how much effort it would take to push a ton of metal around if you weren't using all of the operating parts of the vehicle. You may be doing that in your own life by dragging around old ideas, beliefs and habits. The density of limitation is heavy.

I am going to challenge you to strengthen your muscle of awareness. It's going to hurt but you are going to like it and ask for more because you are strong. And more will come. I will witness your growth with a smile on my face and with a sweet giggle of delight in my heart, that you can hear on my podcast. Yes, that's right, I'm going to enjoy seeing you sweat. Perhaps whimper at times. If I am lucky, I may even see you cry. I'll respect every tear and drop of sweat that seeps from your body. I stand in respect for your courage. It is with love and appreciation we all become the new human order.

Remember this is my classroom and it is like a gym but for - your mind, heart, and body. You are training to become the best man you can be. Learning to get to know your feelings is a part of that. I'm not afraid of your feelings, even if you may be. I'm not afraid of your purity expressed as sensitivity. In fact, I want it. Our world needs it. I appreciate and respect your big heart. If you have a big one, I'm going to invite it to come out and play. If you don't have a big heart, I hope to inspire you to make room for mine and the big hearts of others.

Now as I head back to the front of the classroom, I'm going to boldly ask you to go deep with me. To call forth your limitless potential and to give up your false realities painted on the surface of life. The habits that have distracted and hypnotized you like sheep. And driven you to become hamsters on a wheel going round and round, repeating the same patterns of limitation. It's time to see the diversions that have kept you from your life purpose and heart's desire. Operating business void of heart and acclimating you to pain and suffering in the form of unhealthy relationships, abuse of power, over-extending yourself, addictions and denial of what lights you up - is now up for change.

Have you been a naughty, naughty man? I was once ignorant and blind to it all too. The distraction, dehumanization, and disconnect are things we all must wake-up to. It's ugly what we allow ourselves to participate in but it must be seen in order for change to happen. We must become the solution to the problem by becoming the best version of who we are in our individual lives.

Consider me the messenger and the voice of the heart. That means I will bring attention to your body as well. For some of you, it requires better maintenance. In short, life as we know it is being re-scripted. The sooner you get on board - the better. Instead of waiting for a catastrophe (cue the virus and all the propaganda) in your business, health, or close relationships; join me by taking part in becoming more aware and awake in the world today. That independent responsibility will determine the leaders of our tomorrow as personal self-mastery defines our future. Those are the men who are in my classroom.

Go from Ordinary to Extraordinary:

When you choose to become your highest and greatest potential you have the opportunity to go from ordinary to extraordinary. When you do make that choice, you will get to see just how powerful your free-will is. That is why I learned to choose my thoughts and discovered how important it is to plant empowering intentions in my mind each day.

That's right! You get to take responsibility for your life and direct it with your free-will toward the greatest version of you. You become a creator in a universe of new possibilities. You will come to see how much you are supported and guided when you bring your entire operating system online. That's a big deal.

The process of self-discovery means you also get to weed out the disempowering thoughts as you plant the new seeds of empowering thoughts. You may not yet understand how influential it is to choose your thoughts. It's a lot like investing. Your intentions or affirmations are where you put your money.

I can't emphasize enough how different life is when you are guided by the innate wisdom of your infinite spirit versus habitual living. I do use interchangeable words like: Inner Spark, True Self, Source, Spirit and Higher Self. Choose whatever works best for you.

What we are doing is bridging from feeling like a victim to being a creator of our own reality. That is a metamorphosis of the mind, heart and body. It is an upgrade in frequency that I'm helping your mind to understand. By consciously choosing to live your highest and greatest potential you set into motion your desire to align with your Higher Self as a way of life of the highest standard.

It also gives you the opportunity to see what's keeping you from your greatness. When you gain sight of those things they can begin to fall away. The removal of those obstacles leads to greater possibilities. In other words, I am asking you to go all the way with me boys. To reach for the gold.

It's not easy to see things in ourselves that are hurting and limiting us but it's necessary. No matter what situation you find yourself in, it is the power of your thoughts that got you there. When I point out things that you have ignored about your body or heart, don't think that I am shaming you. I am a coach and it's my job to expect and command your highest performance. If you need a metaphorical smack of clarity on the butt - I'm your gal. Now grab your notebook or iPad and get ready to take some notes. I'll be leaning against the front of my desk, facing you in my black pencil skirt, white blouse and black heels. Once I see that you are ready, I will head to the chalkboard.

Chapter 3
Living Intentionally

Is a part of mind management. This new way of living authentically began with me setting daily intentions. I choose my thoughts based on a higher standard of performance. These changing times are requiring us all to step up. Living intentionally is the beginning of living by choice.

Many have been leading without the whole of what makes them human and that's not going to work any longer. This first step in telling your mind what to think is instrumental in making a shift. It also serves as an activation of our unused potential. Managing my mind began by setting my intentions.

Intentions or affirmations are your daily investment in you. I would suggest the following, if you wish; "I am living my highest and greatest potential." The next intention is a supportive statement that can be added and adapted. "I am guided, respected, provided for, happy and healthy, every day and in every way." These are two new lyrics you can begin humming in your mind. Or you can simply repeat them out loud, over and over again. Treat them like a brand-new song you can't stop singing. Say them a minimum of 10 times each morning. Go for 20 or more, throughout your day.

The most important thing to note is - you do not need to know all of the future steps in advance. You only need to set your new direction into motion. The rest takes care of itself as a form of guidance. You are simply casting your line into the depths of your unused potential.

Just like putting an address into your GPS. The directions will tell you when to make the next turn when the time comes. You trust it will guide you. This is no different. Intentions are a key to turning on your high-performance vehicle. They will begin to direct your life; one turn and one step at a time.

There's more to know about your operating system but before we go there let's get this down. Read or write these intentions each day for thirty days to make it a habit. Continue on after that as they will feel more natural. You don't need to know the outcome in advance, but you do need to plug the intentions into your internal GPS each morning. Men tell me that they are good at taking direction. Your job will be to pay attention to the direction you receive as guidance.

This new daily habit of setting your intentions is as important as brushing your teeth each morning. If you haven't read them out loud several times by the time you've reach your tooth brush, begin circulating them in your mind with your bristles, when you do brush your teeth. These specific intentions never grow old. They serve a great purpose and can be your daily staples. Feel free to add your own intentions over time.

Please write the intentions in your notebook, journal, planner, iPad or smartphone now. You can also write an additional copy on a notecard or a post-it and stick them on your mirror. Make sure they are in a place where you can be reminded each day of the new data you are downloading. Placing a separate copy of them in your car is helpful so that you can continue to consume them as you drive to the office or to an appointment.

Intentional living is a daily practice. That means I expect you to do them each morning like a set of push-ups. Consider this your first new exercise. Remember, I am just like a personal trainer but the heart, mind and body (and soon your lungs) are all on board. There is no reason you can't do this exercise every morning. Pretend it's our time together.

When you begin this work, the hardest part may be managing your mind that keeps wanting to think about other things, or insists it needs to know every step in advance to accomplish the intentions. Just notice what you are thinking and pivot to focusing on your intentions. The guidance will come when the time is right. Remain rooted in your new intentional foundation. Don't run off and get distracted by your thoughts of worry. An unmanaged mind is the old way of being which is: slow, controlled, limited, and predictable. You are moving to a new standard of performance so just notice those other thoughts. I'm teaching you something much deeper than you realize so stay with me boys. We are taking one step at a time. There's nothing to figure out. Other than arranging your morning to include the exercises. This isn't about trying. This is about doing. Just do it.

Bookend your day with another new habit of gratitude. Write a list of 10 things you are grateful for. Be it your health, the sun, your partner, a new client, your kids, new healthy eating habits, or becoming more aware. It's easy to come up with 10. If you aren't making any time to focus on what you are grateful for that ends now. You are missing out on life itself if you don't stop to be thankful. Slow down and smell the roses before the thorns prick you for ignoring them.

Keep a notebook for these gratitude's so that you write them and see them daily. I realize these are very basic tasks I'm asking of you. Just do them. When you get into bed review them in your mind before going to sleep. Smile about the things that feel good. Your gratitude list can be as long as you wish but a minimum of 10. The most important part is to do it daily, and pay attention to the things you value. These exercises aren't up for debate. Don't be lazy and skip either one of these bookends. They hold what comes in the center and serve as a foundation. The creaminess that will ooze in the center will come - once you are no longer controlled by what is repressed.

This about mind management. Any leader out there knows how important it is to manage the mind. These exercises require you to take responsibility and to be the disciplined CEO of your life to accomplish them. They may have to replace 3 - 10 minutes of worry or television, and that's okay. You are in the process of creating new healthy habits to support your growing awareness. I appreciate you making time and raising your standards. I believe in you.

We are barely into the book and you already have gems that will reap rewards. You may not realize how powerful it is to affirm empowering thoughts. However, I suspect you do know that the contents of your mind can weaken and worry you. Your mind is like a computer and it has been busy thinking unconscious thoughts that control your life. You've been programmed on a survival network of density and limitation. Those thoughts will go away as you wake-up and see them.

The manipulation of human consciousness has the majority of the population under a comma of conformity. People's minds are moving so fast they don't even know what they are thinking. They are programmed and operating out of habit. Dependent on outer authority to tell them what to think. There's no creative flow in that way of living. It's a robotic motion of performance. I'm speaking from experience. I was once a robotic sheep in the herd. I understand. I would have never gained sight of my habitual, negative thoughts had I not learned to intend, reflect and breathe. Once I could see them, they no longer had the control they once had. Eventually they fell away.

When you stick with these exercises, you will go from the thinker to the perceiver. That is where the creator in you lies. You'll discover lies you've been told. And how much has been learned upside down or backwards. One of the biggest lies is "seeing is believing." That statement in itself removes creativity from the act of creation. The truth is - perceiving is the first step, and then creation begins to take form. We only get to "see" after something has been created. Seeing is believing was taught backwards. One must believe or perceive first.

That is why we are beginning with intentions. Perceiving that which we wish to create is our first step. You don't see the results yet. You perceive what is possible first. At the end of the day, you learn the feel-good state of gratitude. Feeling is an instantaneous expression of information. It magnifies what you perceive and lifts your frequency. That expedites the power of creation. In other words, there's a lot of fuel for your high-performance engine in these bookend exercises. I toast to your morning intentions and evening gratitude's. You got this!

Chapter 4
Breathing is Key

I love hearing you breathe. Breathing is required in my classroom and gym because you are getting into shape. I'm going to make you sweat. Learning how to breathe more deeply is the key to: stillness, relieving stress and mind management. Not shallow breathing - the slower, the deeper, the better.

Learning to breathe down into your belly is one of the most important exercises I can offer you. Mind management is about noticing when your thoughts are running you. I found breath to be helpful and revealing. When you breathe you want to aim for your belly which contracts your diaphragm when you breathe deeply. The diaphragm is the principal muscle of respiration. It's like an arch that you can imagine erecting and strengthening when you breathe.

Although breathing is what keeps us alive, we all have room for improvement. In both the inhale, and in the relaxing exhale of letting go. When you begin the practice of breathing more deeply you will see how shallow your breath is. It takes concentration to learn to slow down and expand your breath.

Let me help you learn to breathe more deeply. Since I can't stand next to you to hear you breathe, you can imagine me calmly standing next to you. On your inhale slowly expand your belly until your lower lungs are full of air. Then hold that breath for a moment. On the exhale actively engage your abdominal muscles to empty out all of the air. Try that a few times right now as you read.

As your teacher and trainer, I would like you to do this exercise every morning. That way your body and mind remember how important this is to carry throughout your day. You can sit up in your bed and do a set of 10. These breathing exercises can begin after you've said your intentions. Those are meant to start flowing through your mind the moment you wake up. That's the best time to plant your first intentions - the moment your mind wakes up. Rein it in!

When you move onto your breathing exercises you may sit in a straight back chair if that's more comfortable for you. Keep your spine straight. This is when you'll notice if your lower ab muscles are weak or strong. My teacher instructed me to meditate by sitting on a chair without leaning against the back of it. That made me aware of how weak my lower back and lower abs were. Both are stronger now thanks to my meditation/breathing practice and daily 3-minute plank.

Once sitting, keep your spine straight, shoulders down, arms rested on your thighs, chin down, eyes closed and focus only on your inhale and exhale. If your chin tilts upward pull it back down to keep your neck and spine long and straight. A healthy spine is an excellent investment. This exercise will help you become more aware of your posture.

Notice if you shrink your neck down. Pay attention to pulling those shoulders down and keeping your neck long. That requires you getting into your abs. Men in their late 50's and older have a tendency to have squashed necks or rounded upper backs. It's their addiction to feeding their minds and forgetting about the rest of their bodies. They are often looking down and don't hold their shoulders back or chest broad. You can change a rounded, upper spine and stuffed neck if you start changing your poor posture habits today. Reverse aging is available to those who believe and take the healthy steps to care for their body's limitless nature.

Notice as you are breathing can you access your feelings? What does your body feel like when you engage your abs? Can you feel the strength? Can you use your breath to breathe in happiness? Remember that happiness is a choice and not a result of a particular outcome. It's more common to see men looking serious or angry. Happiness is a state of mind. It's there for the taking. I would like to see more men smile. We as ladies deserve a smile. You can obsess about worry or you can use your mind to uplift and inspire your life and others. Where do you want to invest?

Now that you are in your breathing position. Practice as you read this so you can listen to your own breath. Notice your body signals as you do this. Begin by breathing in through your nose. That allows you to take deeper breaths and to engage your lower lungs. Notice if you are straining your neck or other areas of your upper body when you breathe. Instead of putting pressure where it is not meant to go, take the breath all the way down into your belly.

The reason why most people are shallow breathers is because their busy minds control their lives and their bodies movements.

You are learning to take more control of your mind and body by becoming aware of both. Deep breathing will assist your body in taking in more oxygen which benefits the blood and nervous system.

Breathing will also assist you in becoming more **present.** When you are more present you are a better listener. Not only will the people in your life benefit but you will benefit by learning to hear the guidance in the silence. The zero-point stillness within you is a target you want to reach. Plus, there's nothing quite like a man who is present. It makes everything about him more attractive, at least in my eyes.

I understand we were all taught that it was normal to ruminate on the past and to worry about the future, but that is not true. Being right here, right now, in the present moment - is the life of an enlightened man. The perceiver I spoke about earlier can only show up in the present moment. If you don't make space or time to be in the present moment there's no way to hear guidance. Your thinking mind isn't meant to run the show. There's much more to who you are. Once you get out of your head and into your body you'll see.

Now let's pretend we are in the gym right now. When I say, "Give me 10!" That will mean I want 10 slow, deep breaths from you. That might be as difficult as 100 crunches when you first start but it will become easier and more enjoyable over time. You'll easily go over 10 because it feels so good when you get into the zone.

I'm going to give you an easy rep to work with called 7/7/7+ breathing. Begin with an inhale while counting to 7. Hold that breath for a new count of 7. Then exhale for 7+. Typically, it's easier to exhale for far longer than the inhale but for beginners that isn't always the case. I've asked newbies to tell me their inhale and exhale count and I have been told 3. Be gentle with yourself and go to the number you can comfortably reach. Don't force it. You will naturally expand your lungs over time. This isn't about going fast. It's about observing and noticing.

Breathing is vital to our health and well-being. Deep breathing is one of the best ways to lower stress. I would like you to start your day with 10 deep breathing exercises. Throughout the day you will add another 10, by doing one here and one there. This is a new habit in the making. You can use each stop signs or traffic lights to do a 7/7/7+.

Other benefits of your breathing exercise will show up in your meetings when you clearer and more present. It will help you learn to break the habit of thinking ahead while someone else is talking. Men do it to me all the time. I feel them go off in another direction or they try to end my sentence. It sidetracks me because they take me in their direction, and not where I was headed. Another habit is when they nod their head when I've not even made a point yet. They assume they know what I'm going to say. They can't know because I only know as it comes to me in the present moment. That's because my hearts wisdom guides me and speaks through me. Which is different from the logic of mind. In other words, you don't realize how much you are dominating things with your mind and steering conversation, instead of allowing and receiving what is in front of you - in the present moment.

Hopefully, you will begin to catch yourself jumping ahead. That may be your own unconscious fear of the present moment. Allowing, trusting, and receiving can land when blocking, deflecting, and controlling move away. I suggest you begin to observe your habits to gain sight of them. I find it mature, professional and considerate when someone stays present with me. Personal mastery is superior to the rushing, monkey minds of the soon to be past.

Before you go to bed at night, give me another set of 10 breathing exercises to send a message to your brain and body that it's time to relax and let go. You can think about your gratitude's for the day as you drift off. Breathe in the things you are grateful for and breathe out the things you are letting go of. You don't have to focus on what you are letting go of. Let the breath carry it away. Your wiser or Higher Self knows what to clear out.

Another important observation about breathing is that it's the process of contraction and expansion. The push and pull of life is essential to our growth. It is energy moving. The lungs are an example of that, and have been associated with self-esteem and respect for ourselves and others. By learning to breathe more deeply we strengthen our muscle of awareness and we gain sight of our unconscious thoughts.

Consider it an act of self-love as you breathe knowing you are sitting in the Captain's chair of your body. It's a position of power to see our thoughts and to become more present in our life. Breathing is a vital ingredient to our change and transformation. Not to mention all of the health benefits that go along with deep breathing. Gaining a birds-eye view of ourself and life - is the place we want to be.

Think to yourself, "I feel and look younger and healthier when I breathe deeply each day." This serves as an additional reminder of your breath work, until it becomes a weapon of choice that you wouldn't leave home without. Breathing is a superior mind management tool. Use it like the superhero you are.

Gentlemen, I appreciate and respect the efforts you are putting forth to develop these new healthy habits. Your intentions, gratitude's and slow deep breathing will make you more present (and irresistible). There's absolutely nothing sexier than an aware man, in my eyes. Since I can sense a man's presence (as most women can) be prepared for that moment. I'll know if you have been doing the work on yourself. You can't hide a messy room and you can't hide a messy mind. On that note, let's all take one, slow, deep breath together and head to the grill.

Chapter 5
Overthinking is Like Burning a Good Steak

What's that smell? Before I give you the third exercise, let's go further into the depths, my courageous, cuddly, handsome lions. Feel me rubbing up against you affectionately. Hear me giggle. Imagine me tossing my hair and flashing a big smile at you. In appreciation for your courage and participation in this much needed change. I want you to feel appreciated and to sense the hunger in me for your presence. From that place, may I stoke your strength to reach for more?

Let's begin by getting more familiar with the heart. I'll get to the mind in a minute. In the meantime, men have said to me they aren't trained to hold feelings or to listen to the truth of what women go through daily. By joining me, between these pages all of that changes because you are learning to listen by slowing down your mind. The heart has a chance to be heard when you slow down and see more. In time, you will learn to sense the difference of heart over mind as you develop your emotional IQ.

I believe that an underdeveloped emotional intelligence is the result of putting all your eggs into one basket. You know how to diversify your investments. I'm asking you to do the same with your physical, mental, emotional and spiritual well-being. The difference in this diversification is about investing in your relationship with yourself. Which means getting to know your heart a whole lot better. When you discover how efficient and clear the heart is, you'll realize you have eyes to see and ears to hear life in a much more satisfying and authentic way.

The natural ingredients of what created us have been characterized as bad, weak and unnecessary. Nothing could be further from the truth but society did an excellent job manipulating us to believe many limiting thoughts, images and views about our body and about life. They washed away our innate characteristics of innocence/purity, compassion and creativity to enforce a narrative that successfully distanced us from our true nature. That is why I am asking you to command your inner superhero strength, by engaging your free-will to choose to unplug from the hypnosis and to re-script life as you know it - by turning on your high-performance vehicle.

An awake and aware heart would not create the violence and suffering we see in the world today. Those are learned behaviors and beliefs that were deemed acceptable and normal. Yes, we do experience pain but there is far more peace, pleasure and power in us to create a life that we have yet to see. By choosing to listen to our hearts and our body signals we can move into something brand new. The disharmony that currently exists today doesn't make sense when you return to living in a balance of mind and heart.

Most people are blind to the fact that they are stepping on their own hearts and the hearts of others out of societal conditioning and habit. People are teaching their kids to do the same without even realizing it. They bury their faces in denial and become numb to the essence of who they are as their parents stay in relationships and jobs that do not express love, creativity, happiness or inspiration.

People have gotten comfortable with struggle and the constant "doing" and pushing to keep up with the daily stresses of life. Our standard of living has been put further out of reach by an outer authority that has been in control of that lack and limitation narrative. I'm waking you up from that program for you to upgrade your life.

I believe what helped lock many of us into our minds was directing people outward, instead of inward. Leading to over-developed minds that have been credited as superior. The mental body is only one factor of what makes us human. Like the ignition of our car, I mentioned early. The key turns on the mind of the car but there is more required to operate it.

That "more" that I am speaking about beyond the mental body, are the emotional, physical and spiritual bodies that make up our human existence. The mental body has kept some of the smartest of men in an unmovable place. They became so certain that there is no room for something new. It is more important for them to be right than to be happy. There is no wiggle room for a new possibility when you are certain that you know the only way. Creativity cannot flow into a space that says it doesn't exist.

That is why it's not always easy to see where we are playing the game of "fitting in" and turning our back on the heart of who we are. There was little to no education or emphasis on emotional intelligence in our educational system in the United States. We left out an essential ingredient and the most powerful weapon we possess. When we closed off the language of the heart, that speaks as body signals of feeling, we stopped evolving and remained limited. The habit of burning our steak took over, as our way to remove the essential components of who we are, that bring balance and a juiciness to life.

It behooves you to learn how to access the hearts intelligence. If you want to stop burning your steak. The heart speaks through feelings and it conveys information without words - instantaneously. One of the main obstacles that could be in the way of listening to your heart is the habit of over-thinking. I know that none of you would like to burn a good steak but consider this may be what you are doing - to your heart. When you over-think you trade trust for doubt by burning it on the grill of your mind. It doesn't even exist as an option because it's sizzling at the bottom of your grill. Your heart awareness is up in smoke.

When you are in the habit of overthinking, your logic or mind is cooking away heart wisdom - in its fight to figure things out. No trust in that. Emotional IQ is about remembering emotions are good and that they can be trusted. They can actually take you somewhere that your mind can't go.

Do you think Tesla used logic to bring in the ideas he captured about energy? Sure, he used his rational mind to write down his insights but it wasn't his thinking mind that brought them into form. Would you consider that he tapped into the quantum field of consciousness to bring forth that revolutionary information? You'll be amazed at what's in the heart when you learn to listen.

I know each one of you has had some experience in your life where you received information beyond your logic and reason - and you listened. You may have been a child and your innocence allowed you to listen. Without your rational mind getting in the way and talking you out of following your instincts. That information came through feeling and sensing.

The reason I took you back to the womb earlier was for you to remember your foundation because it's a part of you. The purity and surrender of who we are is golden. There's no ulterior motive to harm or hurt someone in that part of us. It's a clear radar system.

We are in the process of bridging into a new way of being in the world. It requires a balance of logic and feeling. If you are in the habit of doubting your heart because your mind wants proof and rejects instantaneous guidance and quantum field solutions - become aware of it. I told you I was going to make you sweat. That's because the unfamiliar, the discomfort and the contradiction to what have been told are all normal to be experiencing right now.

What isn't okay is to gloss over the conflict you may be experiencing in a habit to people-please, deny, or to intellectualize life by burying your feelings. That doesn't mean you have to go into rage either. Your feelings matter. It's important to talk to someone who can accept them so that you can process what you are seeing and sensing at this time. We are in the midst of great change. Lots of feelings are coming up to guide us.

The exercises I've offered in this book can help you build your muscle of awareness. They support you seeing where you are cutting off beneficial information to return to dysfunctional behavior. You wouldn't continue repeating unsuccessful habits in your running your business. I expect you to hold the same standards in your personal life. Even if that means an altercation is necessary in order for you to hold stronger boundaries around unacceptable behaviors.

Getting comfortable with the discomfort is a necessary step to moving out of a hard worn habit of burning away something highly valuable. I need you to keep an eye on yourself to see what you are putting on that mental grill before the juice is burnt away. The over-thinking is stalling what the wisdom of your heart is telling you. I bet a part of you is scared to step up and face the unfamiliar to honor what you know in your heart.

What may intimidate you is the speed that comes in an instant when you don't burn that juice away. A sense of "knowing" delivered from your heart is clarity. You may have learned to muffle it out by frying its juice on your mental grill by endless over-thinking, reflection or strategizing. With more awareness you can change that habit by observing the burn.

Replace the non-action of over-thinking or self-blaming with a healthy natural response. The body and heart know what it needs to restore its own sense of Self. When your mind doesn't get in the way by justifying the continuation of non-action. That is why you need to get better acquainted with your body and heart. That is the team that knows what you need to do to restore your own sense of Self based on the way it feels, as you make necessary adjustments.

The logical mind is slow. People have been stuck in limitation which is lack of information. That is why it is far easier for people to believe lies than to believe they have been lied to. When people are more in tune with their heart and body wisdom, they perceive lies and they sense the truth. They know how to say, "No!" Body knowledge, signals or gut instincts are how our spirit (which lives in our heart) communicates with us.

I came to discover my physical body is the spiritual. That is why "feeling" is so important. I see the heart as a telephone of clarity and that network is run on trust. And it is motored by magnetism. No need to overthink that. Let's move on.

I want to help you establish a relationship with your heart by seeing it as the wise man in you. The part of you that "knows" from a place of sensing what is true. **The perceiver in you**.

My advice is to change your thoughts about emotions to realize you may be burning a good steak every day. You may have remained in non-action, self-censoring and become stubbornly unchangeable without realizing it. Emotions are good and can be trusted. When you feel them, ask what they are doing for you? Remember that they hold information so don't run from them or bury them in your body. They can remain stuck in your tissues and will eventually need to come out. That's why healing is to be respected.

When you reframe your mind to remember - emotions are feelings that carry information, you can remain curious about what they are telling you. We know we can control emotions they don't control us, and they don't have to overwhelm us. Look at emotions as information or energy that is carried as a frequency. Since we are made up of energy and we fluctuate in frequency based on our level of awareness, it doesn't make sense to be afraid of emotions. That's like the ocean being afraid of the rain.

Consider emotions energy that is flowing. When they arise within your body read the information. It is a form of intelligence that doesn't need to use words. I personally can feel emotions to my very core but that doesn't mean everyone around me knows that. I can control my response to them. Unless of course, I'm in the ocean or eating something with a texture and taste I can't hide. In those cases, the pleasurable intensity of what I feel does come out of my mouth through the sounds that I make. I may moan, giggle or release my famous squeal.

I think you would agree that some feelings are hard to hold back because of their intensity but that doesn't mean they are bad. We can actually experience emotions without feeling good or bad about them. They are passing frequencies of information merely meant to inform us. It's when we bury them or burn them on the grill of our mind - when they become an issue.

In my opinion, feelings aren't made for the mind to overthink. They are a language of information received through the body to inform. If they've been suck in us for a long time, they do need to come out and it can feel uncomfortable but it's only temporary discomfort.

Be curious as to where the emotion or feeling takes you. Our job is to listen. The habit of over-thinking has kept many good men from knowing their heart and body more intimately. It's also created non-action and kept unhealthy and even abusive dynamics in place. I'm giving you visuals that comes with a sense of smell (burning a steak) to stoke your memory. I also bring in the visual of the wise man in you for you to befriend that part of yourself. The 007, or superhero you cannot fully show up without your invitation. Your free will used in your daily intention and slow breathing will give him the invite and grilling space - to cook your steak just right.

Let's close out the chapter with a visualization of the wise man in you. Take a deep breath and use your imagination to see what he looks like. I will walk you through a short experience to meet him. Let's pretend you have invited him over to your home. You are sitting in your favorite chair and feeling relaxed. He knocks at your door. You take a slow, deep breath before rising up and out of your chair. You walk toward the front door feeling a sense of excitement and curiosity as you pull the door open. There he is standing before you. Look at his strength, comfort and assurance. Invite him in. Watch how he moves. How he carries himself. Look what he's wearing. You can see him as clear as day.

What do you look like as your wise self? Take a moment to color in the details. As you do, I will tell you what I see. His shoulders are back and down. His chest is broad and his spine is straight. He seems taller than you by a tad because of his posture. His face is relaxed and his smile is soft. He looks young and happy. Powerful yet non-threatening. His fierceness makes me feel as if he protects the world just by being alive. His eyes rest in a place of certainty and his grin carries a playfulness. He trusts life and clearly trust's and honors himself. He radiates success and satisfaction. He is you… in your near future. As we bring this visualization to a close, he has an unspoken message for you. I can only hear the part where he says, "Thanks for having me over. I'd like to stay. If you will have me." I will let the two of you carry on from here, and perhaps you'll enjoy a juicy steak together. I'll meet you on the mat in the next chapter.

Chapter 6
Can I Make You Stretch?

And go to third base with me? That's so naughty. Or is it? I'm actually referring to your third and final morning routine exercise and using baseball as a visual. Just to recap, first base happens the moment you wake up while you are still lying in bed. It's your invitation to your Higher Self (the wise man). Second base is your set of 10 deep breathing exercises. To get to third base, I need you slide onto the floor with me.

It's time to limber up boys. I am requesting 3 to 5 minutes of stretching each morning from you. We gotta make room for the wise man. He's not about contraction or busying your mind, he's about expansion and peace. These new moments in your morning that were ruled by old habits, can now become moments of crafting something new. Your muscle of awareness takes center stage when you make the time each morning to do these three exercises.

The body likes to be stretched. This exercise makes room in your mind for new thought and it lubes up your joints too. It also gives you another couple of minutes to practice your breathing as you stretch. More importantly you need to learn to obey your body instead of ignoring it and using it without awareness. Many men are too lazy to stretch. It shows in the way that they walk and think. When a man is in his body with awareness it shows. It's the way he: carries his body, dresses it, grooms it and keeps it healthy or not.

We are forming a partnership between logic and feeling gentlemen so don't fight me on this - just do your stretching for me. There are no exceptions or excuses just get to the floor and slide into third for me. These exercises will improve your overall wellbeing but you need to discover that for yourself by doing them. These new habits are to be done for 30 days until they become a new healthy habit. You continue them because they feel good. I expect 9 months at the very least of applying this to your life. This is about having a healthier relationship with your body. Your mind has all of the attention right now. Our bodies are being transformed to have a much more advanced consciousness. These exercises support you in being better in-tune with your body.

Self-care of the body is essential for the enlightened man because your biology is changing. That care begins with the thoughts you put into your mind, the air you pump into your lungs and the mobility of your limbs. We no longer need to believe we grow old and become immobile. We can become youthful and vibrant by what we put into our minds and bodies. Move beyond the mental chatter and enter the heart and body to see how much more there is to who you are.

We will consider your morning workout like a ball-field. I can only go to third base with you. Only you can take it all the way home baby. If you have a yoga routine and already know a downward dog, pigeon pose for your hips and other leg stretches for your calves, gluteus, shoulders and hamstrings by all means please do a condescended version. If you don't have any stretches that you already know from physical therapy, a trainer or yoga, look up a 5-minute floor body stretch video and follow along.

These exercises are a daily physical routine that reflects your commitment to aligning with your True Self. They support a healthy self-care regimen that every aware man will benefit from. Take it from a woman who sees men every day. It's not okay to hit 40 or 50 years old and to stop caring for your body. The poor posture from crunching your neck is not a good look for you. Neither are big bellies or arms with no form. That is a life of a man who lives in his mind. That doesn't mean there aren't active men who are strong from the waist down. Where's the balance in that? I've seen herculean calves and big round bellies. Why? Men, this is about your entire body waking up to a new version of you.

It concerns me when I see men who are not taking care of their bodies. The lack of impulse control is more apparent when it's an eating or drinking habit that makes men look 3, 6, or 9 months pregnant. Pure visceral fat or a bouncy belly that your doctors don't mention doesn't excuse a better management on your part. Since they don't bring up the connection between your body and Spirit - I will. Get a full-length mirror and take your whole form into account. I'm holding you to a higher standard. I want you to be aware of what you are eating, thinking and what your body is saying to you. I also want you to get to know your lungs better by noticing how deeply you are breathing. The Superhero in you is proud of his form. He honors his body and his posture shows his feel-good self-worth. That's the man I'm calling forth in you.

When you develop a better connection with the wisdom of your body you will know when it's full. You will know when you're not eating the right foods and when you need more exercise and sleep. It's clear when a man is living his life through logic only. There's a disconnect and it can be seen guys. It's that obvious. I'm encouraging you to develop healthy habits and heathy relationship with your body. I have my eyes on you handsome.

These 3 simple exercises have great purpose. The daily intentions motor your unused potential and activate a relationship with the wise man in you. The breathing exercises assist you in more areas in your life than you can imagine, including breaking the habit of overcooking your steak, integrating your emotional and spiritual body and bringing in more much needed oxygen. The stretching makes room for more of your juicy wisdom, increases your flexibility and it helps you to be more in touch with your body signals. Which many of you are currently ignoring when you scarf down food. Slow down! And consider all 3 exercises mandatory energy maintenance of your high-performance vehicle.

Higher intelligence requires higher standards and brings higher performance. As your coach, your daily routine is not to be missed so plan for it and get it done before you even leave your bedroom. It's that important. You may need to get up fifteen minutes earlier or hold off on turning on the television or picking up your phone. If you do not stretch because you pride yourself on being a runner, cyclist, weight lifter or stair climber you are not exempt either. Your tight muscles and your inflexible hips show in the way that you walk. Your Inner Spark is realized in your biology. Your tight muscles aren't making room for more of your super human nature. You gotta realize you are the new advanced technology. It's not going to be about a smartphone or computer. It's going to be about our high-performance vehicle. The one that's covered in skin.

Think of the posture of the wise man from the visualization. The comfort in his body showed. Let me tell you gentlemen, rigid thinking and obsessive worry isn't something you can hide. It shows on your face, how you hold your shoulders and neck, the form of your back, the depth of your breath, the pace of your walk, and the ring around your waistline. All of these areas are indicators of whether you are present in your body or not. If you are invested in worry and have prided yourself on an active mind, I'd like you to strengthen yourself in areas of weakness so that you can hit a home run for me. This is about a new balance. We are taking steps that will allow us to obey our own Spark of Infinity, to bring about a whole new human and way of being. These exercises are both a reminder of our transformation and a conscious participation. The more you listen to your body, the more you'll know what it needs.

Stretching increases your flexibility, improves posture, reduces stress, body aches and it helps in maintaining a range of motion in your joints. I need you to remain open and curious as you transform and that will require flexibility. Please don't let your stubbornness skip right over what I am asking. I expect you to stretch every day. If you need to visualize me blowing a whistle or standing over you with a smile on my face and a timer in my hand - then do it. In the meantime, snap a "before" photo of yourself and a short video of your walk and posture. In nine months, I want to see the man you birthed. Write down the date today and send me before and after pictures so that I can personally congratulate you.

The whole of a human encompasses mental, physical, emotional, and spiritual well-being. This is all housed in the body. That is why **self-care is essential** as it establishes a relationship with the body. Men aren't scrutinized about their physical presence the way that women are but that doesn't stop anyone from noticing unhealthy men. I would like to stretch your mind and your muscles to get more of your vibrant Spirit inside of you. The wise man doesn't slump, isn't rigid, un-groomed or strained by carrying more weight around than is healthy for him. If none of those descriptions apply but your laziness does, then that's your work.

If your body is not a priority, it is now because the Spirit of who you are resides in your biology. Your mind isn't meant to continue to block your fullest potential. If you laugh this off because you believe your bank account is all that matters, I'll have to share something about men who only think about their net worth. It's kind of funny. They are the same men who believe in lack. They never believe they have enough because they have related lack to living. That scarcity consciousness is a never-ending loop. It makes me wonder how they'll handle the future when money ends up not being worth the paper it's printed on one day. But that's for a later date.

When you become more aware you will remember that the greatest things in life are free. You may not spend much time appreciating your body or your close friendships because you are more focused on monetary gain but both are free. The only real gain in life comes from gaining sight of your thinking. That way inherited, antiquated beliefs can fall away, as well as, unhealthy habits that are hurting your body. You'll then begin to see what really matters through your own perception. The unseen will become visible when you make space for its realization within you.

When you round the bases each morning you will start to see thoughts you want to strip out of. You will most likely discover that you bought into the beliefs of lack that contribute to unhealthy behaviors. Notice if your mind thinks "there is not enough:" time, money or resources. Those are some of the programs that replaced our original brick and mortar and put many on the track of a habitual, stress-induced life of lack. It's up to you to make the shift to live in your limitless nature that exists outside of the density of limitation.

We cannot hear our wise self who speaks through our heart and body when our mind dominates. Just because the mind is busy thinking doesn't mean it's accomplishing anything. A speedy mind is always having to catch-up because it believes there's not enough time or resources. That's a part of what keeps the mind running towards something it can never fully have because its foundation rests on lack. We were programmed in limitation. It's time to release those programs.

The structure of lack obsesses on doubt, pessimism and worry. That's not living. That is surviving. I call it enslavement. Programming that I would want to gain sight of in order to remove it. Why wouldn't you want to experience the limitless through your physicality? Realize that we have become entrapped in a false image of ourselves that is tied to limitation and suffering.

So much of what we learned is backwards and untrue. That is why it's probably difficult for you to believe that by slowing down you can actually speed up creation. When you slow down enough you will meet that zero-point energy field within you where optimization exists. That place of stillness is a state of complete balance and pure potential.

Limitation and illness can be overwritten. I have separated and disconnected myself from the belief that my physical experience of myself is flawed, aging or disease ridden. I no longer believe that my body is unable to function optimally at all times. Although I pointed out things about your body to become aware of, I don't think you need to focus on what's wrong with your body. Have a better relationship with your body and listen to its signals to make necessary adjustments. Focus on your physical limitlessness and sense your high-performance potential. What do you want your body to be able to do?

When you tap into your highest and greatest potential there is so much more available than you've been told is possible. Go to third base with me in your imagination, every day, by doing your exercises. Consider the endless possibilities that peace and peak performance can bring. Our new reality is not found in a busy mind. Get onto the highway of infinite intelligence found within; a wealth of wellbeing, clarity and potential await you

Chapter 7
Power of the Heart

It's a power like no other! I know you smart and sexy lions like power. However, this power isn't found in book smarts and doesn't come easy but it is natural. And so is fear. It just depends on how you deal with it. What I learned about fear is that it brings more love. And that's why I want you to face it and go for the gold!

A new skillset is needed to master the realms of the heart. Beyond learning to breath deeper and slower, the art of allowing is its own skillset. Not everything in life is achievable through effort alone. By remaining open, you may discover sensing your emotions doesn't take effort but stuffing them does, and reversing the habit takes time. I would like to encourage you to drop into the softness or purity of your heart and expand your mind at the same time - by going into your fears.

Self-mastery is what I practice and teach. In the emotional empire of the heart, one does not need to block or swallow their feelings. Expressing them isn't easy for everyone. I get it. Although we were naturals at it as kids, we ended up replicating what others told us was safe. That's why some people gloss over their feelings when someone is abusing them. I was one of those people because I was taught to be nice. Not to myself, but to others. We can control our feelings but why would we throw away information from our emotions that tell us something isn't right?

You can better understand emotions when you stop seeing them as weak or unimportant. They are quite the opposite. They are wise and informative. The only weakness is - the fear of them. Or the program that tells you to avoid being honest with yourself, or others, in order to "be nice." That doesn't mean it's okay to unleash in blind rage either. This is a transition for us all, in how we navigate the unfamiliar, the discomfort, and the contradiction to the things we've been told.

To honor the heart is to heal it, listen to it and to balance boundaries. In opening up to my heart I had to feel through some tough buried emotions, and to get uncomfortable with being honest about what worked for me and what didn't. I learned to go from; no boundaries to have firm boundaries. It's now a dance between the two. Laying firm boundaries was tough at first. I had to get to know myself and to let go of people-pleasing habits. Navigating between firm and no boundaries gives me plenty of space to try new things and to say, "No" when something doesn't feel right. If someone is being abusive or manipulative, I speak up for my heart. It's not my job to change them but it is my job to lay boundaries, and to move away from people who aren't willing to be honest with themself or kind to me.

I have learned to listen to my heart by dropping into it but that meant getting out of my mind and into my body. By the way gentlemen, I do love the minds of smart men. Just because I am asking you to be more present and aware of your heart and body doesn't mean I don't appreciate your mind. Your warrior nature comes from your heart. There's a wildness in your heart. Trust me, I found mine and it's not tamable. Look how it now has a stage, a classroom and a gym. All here to call more of your heart to come play with mine. I do love love but I'm not trying to take yours away. I'm merely inspiring the unleashing it. Quite the opposite of a tamer, right?

I respect and appreciate your smart minds. I can lick an intellect like a lollypop. I find it that tasty but couple it with a compassionate heart and you'll have my attention. Men have taught me a lot about the mind through business and my academic degrees. In business, I had the opportunity to golf amazing courses around the world. I negotiated deals with CEO's and managers from every area of industry. Men have brightened my life with their minds. I thoroughly enjoy the company of men and will champion them to the end. That is why I would like to share what I have learned about the heart, since men have taught me so much about logic and reason. I appreciate how much men continue to provide for me. I love men.

I would have never thought I would earn an advanced degree in heart technology by having mine broken so many times. I'm not suggesting that for you. And, no my degree didn't come from a university. It's life that taught me. I want to help you understand the strength, wisdom and power of heart. When the heart breaks it actually grows and expands. That only happened for me when I didn't let my mind win by convincing me to close off to what was on the other side of the pain. Why is pain such a great teacher? Perhaps it's in the friction that creates alchemy. Yogananda once said, "Pain is the prod to remembrance." In my experience there's a push and pull factor that's essential to growth; a contraction and expansion. That's the alchemy that taught me the power to love myself and it took going into fear to get to the other side.

Today it is the greatest knowledge, teaching and practice I possess. The other fascinating characteristic of the heart is its speed of communication. We call that light speed technology - clarity. Our mind can take years, or a lifetime, to decipher something that our heart can know in an instant.

Let's say you are in regular arguments with your partner and are used to looping into unhealthy patterns. If you only use your mind, you can convince yourself to repeat that pattern, over and over again, forever. Same with a job where you are unhappy and unsatisfied in your position. Your mind can convince you to stay. Whereas your heart and its sensory mechanism to feel can instantly convey to you that your situation doesn't feel good. It does that because what's in the heart is important to acknowledge. When you ignore those feelings and continue to argue and remain in the unfulfilling positions, dynamics and situations, you feel your frequency drop. There's a heaviness like a cloud that doesn't go away. That's the density I'm encouraging you to get out of by raising your vibration by listening to your heart.

When you resist listening to your heart pain continues, no matter how clever your logic is. Just because you've been strong enough to ignore it doesn't mean you have conquered anything. You've been superiorly nonsensical and I won't be shaking your hand or patting you on the back for that. You also won't feel good when you continue to ignore those feelings because you are a companion to your heart and that relationship is important. Now you will be more aware of the pain you are causing your body when you ignore it.

Your body signals (gut instincts/goosebumps) are information systems that you may be in the habit of ignoring in order to burn your steak to rationalize life. It's the money, or you think you can control the other person and things could get better in time. There are endless possibilities in the delay tactic toy box of the mind. Just like your body saying "I had enough" but you continue to push it and eat more, over-exercise, stay at an unfulfilling job or continue watching too much television. Stop ignoring your body signals boys!

That logic and reason you give so much credit to continues to trick you into remaining in that 10% (or less) potential. You're not expanding out of that loop. You are staying "safe" in the familiar or in truth of being frightened of your unused potential.

When you consider accessing all of you by including the ability to feel; your awareness expands to accepting the wise man as a part of you. Including him is a step toward truly loving yourself. That may mean facing the temptation (impulse) to turn away from him, to return to your old habits. When you turn away from your heart guidance, you are turning away from the wise man in you. Observe and notice.

Imagine every time that you do this, you move into the slow lane to let your mind: presume, rationalize, analyze, manipulate and control outcomes in your head. Sure, you mind is speeding in that slow lane because it's thinking a million miles per second. It's fooling you that you have it all figured out and are getting so much accomplished. But it's actually looping back to a similar and familiar outcome.

You are getting far less done than you imagine by being in your mind all of the time. Do your exercises and allow yourself to reflect in order to pull things away to give them more space, to see it all more clearly. That space comes from the heart. Not the mind. But don't keep stalling by over-reflecting. There's a balance.

The speedy mind is excellent at distracting you from seeing more. Until you learn the new habit of slowing it down to gain sight of what you are thinking. They may just be a stream of worries. If you are living life in your mind, I want you to take notice. That alone will promote something new. That is your muscle of awareness and I want to see you flex it!

Your mind is a locomotive that may be speeding away from your heart but it doesn't mean the heart goes away. I see the corridors that men intricately construct in their minds that keep them busy in non-action. I wait until I get a chance to respond after two, three, four or five analogies, more data and locomotive stops. In fact, there are so many stops there is often less clarity at the end. Just superb stalling and denial techniques.

Without the heart and its crystal clarity you are most likely in the same loop producing similar results. Results that often include more harm or pain to your body that is trying to guide you. Sure, your doctor said it's a skin issue and never mentioned it has anything to do with you ignoring your body's signals. Even though the skin is your largest organ, he deals only with the symptom, not the source cause. He puts you on anxiety medication to numb out your feelings even more, and maybe a topical ointment. There's nothing heroic in disarming your greatest asset.

Each one of us must tackle the situations and characteristic traits we know are abusive and unacceptable in our personal and professional lives or they will continue to control us. To engage the wisdom in your body you must act on what you sense. Your body communicates with you. Are you listening?

The heart operates on trust. When you learn to employ the heart and not just logic more information is available. The heart holds wisdom in its spaciousness. It knows there is something to learn in every situation. It doesn't justify repeating unhealthy habits. It feels pain and lets you know it cares. It's only the mind that likes to plot, scheme and control.

The heart operates through trust and faith. It is through my heart where I sense everything in life is orchestrated for my highest growth and greatest potential. My heart has taught me that I am not alone and that I am loved and guided, every day and in every way. I no longer carry the weight of the world on my shoulders. I trust life. I trust myself and that required me trusting my heart and my body. They work together to inform and guide me.

When you get confused as this is new territory, pivot to curiosity to explore new areas you have not gone before. For example, let us return to that argument. You are not getting along with your partner and you are in a repetitive cycle. Would you consider the reason you continue to go there is because you are detached from your feelings? Do you need to wait until you realize you have been in pain for a long time before you make a change? How long must you wait?

Have you allowed reason to return you to the same place producing the same unpleasant results? I encourage you to get curious next time. Explore new areas and stop getting stuck in your dramas. Trust that the drama may help you come to a whole new realization at a later point in your life. Make peace with the dramas of your life first - by accepting your responsibility in them. If you are lost in a drama you are typically disconnected from your feelings. Stop getting lost in the dramas by having consideration for your heart. It's letting you know it doesn't feel good. Observe your feelings and allow the information to teach you something to move onto a new outcome. Allowing is the act of receiving. Receive the information and act on it.

What the heart is not - is condescending and co-dependent. To better see what the heart is, let's see where it could be hidden by the mind. I have observed highly intelligent men, unconsciously and perhaps consciously, using their intellect to bully curiosity. Some men proudly display an attitude of arrogance, others practice isolation, as a result of their condescension. They can do this with humor or with anger or take the isolation route and not interact with others at all. Either way, publicly or silently, they justify their behavior by blaming others ineptitude. They make no apology for thinking others are stupid and beneath them. I see their behavior like rubbing the spirit of someone into the ground like a cigarette. Putting out the flame of another to appear superior is not heart. No emotional connection is available for other people in your life when you choose mind over heart.

I see condescension as a clever and unconscious heart-blocking technique. When there's no developed emotional intelligence it shows in the habit of hurting those around you and never taking responsibility. Kids don't bond with Dad's in a healthy way when there's a lack of heart connection. Then they often take on the unconscious habit to be like their Dad to get the bond they longed for. We can't make people become what we need but we can be that to ourselves when we listen to our heart. Those of us who choose to rise up must continue to tackle the character traits and situations we know are abusive and unacceptable in our personal lives to change them.

Patriarch displayed many abusive attitudes and behaviors that were seen as the gold standard and a sign of intelligence. I'm telling you there's nothing golden about bullying or abusing power. And that's why we must make changes within ourselves to discontinue what our ancestors started. Men who are in the practice of arrogance based on knowledge, trade their compassion for dominance. That's not attractive, it's ugly. Its mind winning over heart. In my classroom and gym that is sloppy, ignorant and immature.

Have you traded heart for mind? Put all your eggs in one basket? You can now have a balance of both by learning the language of feeling. It's actually the first language you spoke as an infant. In order to break a natural habit of feeling you learned to think more. It may be why men love analogies; a never-ending search for more data? One may be enough. I value clarity, as well as, storytelling. An overuse of analogies, after an answer has been made clear, is a good way to lose your audience. For me, I feel my vibration spiraling down into the slow lane of mental masturbation as I am left out of the conversation and the topic becomes pulverized. You know when someone doesn't even notice that it's no longer a conversation because they are too busy walking down those long corridors in the back alleyways of their mind. That's what they created to get away from their heart and why the steak is burning.

I see how common it is for men to have done this in their own minds to deflect from going to the heart of the matter. You can either go into your limitless potential or can keep up the habit of diversion. It's not efficient in my eyes, and yet most men value efficiency. Men even invest in cars with speed but don't always employ their own high-performance vehicle. If you like luxury and speed learn to operate your mind and heart to hit that highway of infinite intelligence.

Once you develop your muscle of awareness you can observe and even pivot toward curiosity and try on something new. That in itself is a heroic step that leads to change. As you awaken you become more attuned. You discover that you are learning to rid yourself of unnecessary fears and outdated beliefs and habits. The magnetism in your heart is a tool not to be clouded by your mind. Your avoidance of going into the fear that keeps your habits in place is what is keeping you from more love. Let's get that vibration up and notice when the volume of it goes down. Don't let your mind keep you there. I know you like to rise up. I want you to go for the gold to get your real power because our world needs it. I meant it when I said, "I need you."

When you employ the power of your heart things change. It takes time, and daily discipline of a higher standard. When you move through this process there are shifts and pivots to make. Notice your body signals whether they strong or less strong they are your guidance system. You will know when your muscle of awareness is getting stronger when you notice your behaviors, whether you acting defensive, people-pleasing, condescending, or anxious. Also notice if your thoughts are distracting you so that you can see what is happening, while remaining rooted in your breathing. Don't run away with your thoughts, stay in your body and listen to how its feeling. That is how you establish a new foundation of stability. And return to the present moment and observe what needs to fall away.

By remembering that both - fear and love - are natural; you can use one to help you get more of the other. If I ask you to run down the field of fear and you never look back to catch the pass of love, then you hit the end zone of life with nothing more than your fears. When you allow each and every cell in your body to open and receive directly from your heart, your hands will fly up and your body will jump higher than you ever before - because you want to catch that pass. You want to become all you can be. That's how love wins. Touchdown!

Chapter 8
Stay Open & Curious

You are more playful when you are open and curious. A big part of me becoming aware was about learning to fall in love with myself. What does that have to do with you or your business? A lot! I'm just beginning to wet your lips and massage your mind with new ideas and perspectives that lead to a much more fulfilling and satisfying life. I respect and appreciate your willingness to be open and curious with this coursework of life.

Falling in love with myself required loving the parts of me others shamed away and said were: bad, defective, wrong and unacceptable. Those are the parts of myself I learned to dislike because I was told they were unlovable. You have done the same to parts of yourself too. I was too young to know better and maybe you were too.

It may sound like an easy thing to love yourself. It wasn't for me because I had learned the opposite. Once I discovered the unconscious thoughts that had been thinking me, I became aware of what was fueling my locomotive. No matter how confident many appear on the outside there is a lot of disharmony happening on the inside. That's what this work will clean up.

Despite being a quiet, kind, little girl who grew up to become a kind, people-pleaser of a woman the program of "being nice" was about how I was treat others, not myself. I discovered my unconscious thoughts and beliefs, all of which I absorbed as a child, were not very kind at all. Putting others before myself was a narrative that had nothing to do with self-love. And many people are doing the same thing in their lives too. They learned self-hatred or a form of it. That's why learning to love myself was so hard. I had mastered quietly hating or judging myself. Personal mastery was about reversing everything. This is why I say we learned things backwards.

Once I gained site of my negative thoughts, I had to put down my armor to get into the softness of my heart to rescript my life and that wasn't easy. Ignorance was bliss. Self-mastery was for the warrior in me. I had to be brave to move out of the box of conformity and become uncomfortable with trying something new. It seemed selfish to tend to my own needs and to discover my own desires. That's why it's valuable to remain open and curious. Blowing the mind isn't fun but it is liberating.

Other people in my life weren't modeling behaviors that I was attempting to try on. Which made moving out of the box even riskier. I didn't know what I was doing outside the norm. But I did come to experience why people don't leave the herd. Becoming a person who isn't a replicate of what society deems acceptable is scary. And as a result, I've become fearless by leaving the pack. I found an inner freedom that I call My Higher Kingdom and now I'm inviting all of you to come play with me in your kingdom too.

The part of my mind that had been built to people-please; placed more merit on what other people thought of me than what I thought of myself. That had to change once I saw through meditation exactly what I thought of myself. Only through self-love could I alchemize self-hatred. The rewards came every time

I went into the burn of vulnerability and found more of my soft, pure, sensual spirit. Over time I stepped more into my authentic self that looked nothing like the image's others forced on me.

I would like to support you in doing the same. One-step and one aspect of you at a time that has been forgotten. The parts of you that deserve to be loved and to know it's safe to love and feel again.

Loving myself required making mistakes and taking risks just like you do in business. I went through fear and anxiety but I allowed myself to feel into the discomfort until I got to the other side of the pain. Hiding there were aspects of me only I could embrace by remaining open and curious.

Quite honestly, there were a lot of fears I had to face. That is why I know what it takes to become fearless. Feeling the burn that told me it's unsafe to be vulnerable but still walking into it the feeling without letting it stop me is how I alchemized fear into love. The "land mind of illusion" takes a courage to conquer its facade. And, I didn't even know I had courage. After years of being identified as a shy and submissive female I had no idea a lioness was inside of me. One who would call forth an army of lions, with my wide-open heart, is not who I expected to become. I'm amazed, ecstatic and inspired by my own life and by the lives of every man who rises up with me.

This is why I advise you to remain open and curious. Instead of running toward a coping mechanism that could be over-eating, over-thinking and numbing out on things that distract you. Apply your breathing and stay with the feeling that arises. I have found that by going into my fears there's something completely different on the other side. Just keep breathing and paying attention to your breath. Anxiety isn't fun to feel but knowing there is something on the other side is a reason to remain open. You may have been trained to shield yourself from your own pureness. You've hidden that part of you to remain safe in a world that told you; illness, pain and suffering is the image of your body and of life. I would have never realized that my sensual nature was a part of my purity had I not remained open and curious.

Your blind spots may be in your comfortable and predictable, repetitive behaviors that end in you blaming someone or something for your anxiety, misery, unhappiness or contention. I understand it's difficult to take an honest look at ourselves and to stop blaming others for misery and unhappiness in our lives. We have the power to end the unhealthy behaviors and situations in our life. Becoming conscious and aware means you see your part in everything you create. You take responsibility and give up playing the role of victim and we move out of enslavement. We are now upgrading our technology.

It's an act of self-love when you bring an end to your dramas and unhealthy habits. The liberating piece is that you are the only one who can set yourself free and move into your unused potential. Mastery involves taking the lessons and the love and moving forward with openness and curiosity. Life becomes an exploration.

Aren't you curious about aspects of yourself that you left behind? That may have been considered different or unacceptable. Maybe you saw your sensitive heart as unmanly because a misinformed world taught you to conform and that domination was natural. I'm sorry you were lied to and that you were shamed for being yourself. Healing is to be respected as a process we move through to upgrade our bodies technology.

By building a relationship with my emotional body I was able to embrace the authentic aspects of myself. My feelings were important for me to befriend in order to heal my heart and to forgive myself. It's one thing to forgive those who mistreated us but the bigger work is often in forgiving ourselves. No one can give us the kind of love we truly long for as adults, other than ourselves. But life doesn't teach us that because it directed our power outward and not inward.

When you stick with your daily exercises and face your triggers by realizing your emotions are drawing your attention to something to take note of, you will reap the benefits and discover the treasures once discarded as trash. Keep remaining open and curious like a young boy. When you listened to your instincts as a child and moved toward things that felt good because disharmony registered as unpleasant. Go back to remembering feelings were an indicator that guided you. See all emotions as sources of information and that you don't need to get lost in any one of them.

If you discover you are disliking yourself, observe what parts of yourself you are bullying. Use your imagination to put your arms around the boy that was bullied. You could even put your arms around your own chest and picture hugging him. Your observation alone is not unlike discovering something in your business that is impeding your success. You are happy to know what's been costing you profits because you can do something about it. This is no different. Personal development directs that same level of attention toward the things that aren't working. That is the only way they will change.

I am inviting you to get hot and sweaty with me because alchemy requires heat to transform. That's exactly what I'm in the business of doing... heating you up! As a woman of transformation, I understand the value of friction. We are here to evolve and your mind doesn't have to understand it all. You are far more in your limitless nature as a multi-dimensional being than you are mired in limitation. Bust out of that density by remaining open and curious and come with me.

With breath and curiosity, you can come to realize it's not the situation that's causing the anxiety - it's the thoughts you are thinking. The thoughts may have been established when you were a child and it's time to heal them. Whip open that button down shirt and show me the inner Superhero in you that can turn fear into love. That may mean allowing the situation to inform you that it's time to renegotiate with those in your life based on what you now know is true for you.

When you are triggered it's okay to let that part of yourself know that you are safe and that your feelings are valid. Don't go into over-thinking go into loving yourself. Be there for your heart. And be that heart by letting the innocence and purity in you know - it is safe to be here now. You no longer need to escape the body to hide in your mind. Self-censoring is an old pattern we are all moving out of. It's time to be honest with yourself even if those around you can't be honest with themselves.

I'm inviting you to become the Master of your reality by getting into your body and falling in love with your own heart. When I slowed down my thoughts, I was able to see things I was thinking like, "I'm not safe. I am going to die. I'm in trouble. Something is wrong with me. I'm a failure. I'm no good. I don't deserve to be loved. I made a mistake and I'm going to be punished. I'm not good enough. It's not safe to be here." Curiosity and breathing were important for me to observe my fears and to ultimately alchemize them into love.

It's important to realize that our thoughts are patterns of behavior. They aren't who we are. In fact, discovering who I was not was the biggest step in discovering who I was. That is how the old falls away by seeing the untruth. Once I saw the silent hell within me, I layered on intentions to expedite my process because I realized my mind believed those thoughts. I took an active role to rescript my mind while the old fell away. I even applied intentions to tell myself like: "I love myself. I take responsibility for what I create. I remain open and curious. I learn ways to honor and love myself more. I forgive myself for being so hard on myself."

Instead of "trying" to fix uncomfortable situations by thinking I was responsible for other people's feelings, as codependency once taught me, I came to realize that loving myself was top priority. When I learned to honor myself others could honor me too. There's was no need to people-please or unconsciously manipulate, control, or strategize when I came from a place of honor. All of those behaviors were unconscious and exhausting. What I discovered was that when we love and respect ourselves, others either come along or they don't. The ones that do, respect and trust us more for what we represent as being authentic. Those are the friends and clients who stand by me today. I have plenty of room for more.

I'm inspiring you to something brand new. When you remain open and curious and allow change; you may find that one door closes and another opens. That's okay. That's how change works. Not everyone in our life is going to support us becoming all that we can be. The most important person to get on board is you.

We all do this in our own time but holding onto those who are limiting us isn't self-love. What's important to consider is that the opposite of attachment is self-love. It's a fair trade-off. Trust me. I know it well. I've been learning non-attachment for many years now. There's great freedom here. It's as different as conditional and unconditional love.

When you take responsibility for your own personal growth life becomes far more interesting. When you stop disowning parts of yourself, out of habit, you will have more of yourself to love and to make new choices with. Once you understand how this works; the only thing you will ever abandon again is the bad habit - not yourself. That's another thing we learned backwards. We were all quick to abandon ourselves but not the abusive behavior, unhealthy situation or relationship. You are far too important to leave behind! Allow the space of curiosity and openness to lead you to new places.

I'll share were openness and curiosity took me in the next chapter and even more in Part II. That way you can get to know me more intimately.

Chapter 9
My First Steps to the Plate

And where they led me. Self-realization became my heartfelt goal after reading the book "Autobiography of a Yogi." I wanted what the author and spiritual master Paramahansa Yogananda possessed. That was unusual because I was living the "American dream" and wasn't interested in yogis. I was however attracted to the human potential he had realized. I felt something "different" when I read his book.

For me, realization took on a very different trajectory than I would have ever imagined. It propelled me into healing my past, by working with a psychologist, while incorporating the spiritual disciplines he outlined in his weekly lessons. Those lessons I had signed up for after reading his book took me a year and half to complete.

His teachings broadened my perspectives about my spiritual nature. I inwardly made the decision to use my free-will to awaken my divine will or infinite spirit. Interestingly, I came to discover I knew very little about what that meant. Despite a lifetime of organized religion, I was mired in guilt and shame. In other words, I woke up to my life of enslavement and wanted out. That was no easy feat. Although today, it will be easier for you because of the momentum of change that's here to support the "Great Awakening."

Call it crazy but that spiritual book was as if someone hit me over the head with a brick. I had no choice but to get real with myself and boy I am glad I did. Because I was living as a shell of a human designed by others. I had forgotten the immensely advanced technology of my body. It had been switched off and controlled by the narrative of an outer authority... until that time.

Over ten years, I radically changed from the inside out. Each year was a lifetime unto itself. It's remarkable when I reflect back and think of all of the places, people, workshops, books, knowledge and realizations that came into my life. Many people in my shoes would have given up because of the pain. There was a lot of loss that I faced. The people and the things I loved most fell away. None of it felt good but when I look back now, I see how it was all for my highest and greatest good.

I went through a process of redirecting my will to my highest and greatest potential. I could access clarity on the other side of my fears. As I stated earlier, my mind convinced me that I would die if I went anywhere near my fears, but that turned out to be untrue. The act of feeling through traumas and tough experiences of my past was an important release of stuck energy and an integration of more of my infinite spirit which brought me profound realizations.

When I directed my will through daily intentions and breathing, my rushing mind slowed over time. By choosing to become mindful and applying breath, I was able to choose where I put my attention. My Higher Self led me to new vistas I never dreamed possible, in my former exclusive "rational thought only" led life.

How I made decisions changed because my world opened up and possibilities surfaced that my left-brain would not have permitted. With a sense of imagination and beauty found in my own heart, I was able to tap into my creativity that began to design a whole new life for me. By opening up to my heart, it made sense to make decisions based on my well-being. Instead of what the world said was important. Society no longer told me who I was. My spirit from within showed me.

To discover more of who I wasn't, I began to brave the world through exploration but without faith and trust that would not have been possible. Layers of trust were built as I learned to listen to my intuition. I believe intuition is a feminine attribute that we all possess and is found in heart intelligence. Patriarchal rule may have dismissed intuition because its power to lead us by our hearts desire and purpose - prevents conformity. Along with trust, I had to have faith in my new intentional living and that it would guide me. Learning to trust the wise woman in me was one thing, but to have faith that the next action steps would come when the time was right, was another major adjustment.

I was leaving one way of being in the world, where my mind had been sold a bill of certainty. When I did what outer authority told me to do, I could expect "said" results. That's how they owned my will. Until I realized it was mine, and not up for the taking. They weren't going to have me by the "fear balls" for life. I was determined to go for the gold and free myself.

I now have a healthy relationship with my emotional and physical body. I listen to what it is telling me and I allow myself to nurture my softness or purity with self-care. That's my inner radar system and I'm willing to take good care of it. Somewhere along the way, life eliminated the need for us to nurture ourselves. There's nothing smart about that. Would you not agree?

Our strength is in our softness. Nurturing was an act of creation in our incubation. Whether we denied it in our adulthood or not, it is a part of us. This important characteristic of who we are was forgotten when we devalued the heart. Nurturing is a mature emotional response to our body, that doesn't seek over indulgence by pushing ourselves too much or by being overly lazy.

Making such significant changes in my life, helped me to see that by "doing" for the sake of being busy created stress in my life. That habit "separated" and blocked me from sensing or hearing my inner guidance. When I aligned with my purposeful state of "being" I moved through a reconciliation within myself. That required a whole lot of forgiveness and compassion because I realized I wasn't a very nice person to myself. I didn't have the best teachers in my childhood to know what balance or peace looked or felt like. Therefore, I needed to learn how to reparent myself and to nurture the whole of me. That took an emotional, mental and physical maturity that supported my natural spiritual nature.

My former reality had been void of a loving connection to my own body. I was forced to grow up as an adult when I redirected my will. I went from moving through the motions of life; to learning how to surrender and listen to my instincts/intuition/inner guidance and respond to my gut - which is an act of trust. I also got comfortable with the stillness within me that had more energy than movement.

These were ways that I realized there was a clear plan, and although my mind couldn't see it in advance, the quantum field within me could. At the right time, I would receive the guidance, through my emotional and physical intelligence to take the next step. It took time for me to trust my instincts/advanced technology again, and to have faith in the direction that wisdom was leading me.

The limitlessness of the power that resides in our hearts is magnificent. It's a universe of possibilities that can craft spectacular miracles and magnetize serendipitous connections, that still blow my mind. The proof my former pragmatic and idealistic mind needed in order to move forward on my instincts - limited me. I traded proof for faith and I got miracles. I traded doubt and certainty for trust, and I got the best life ever! Giving my will over to the guidance of my Higher Self or infinite spirit is how I brought my kingdom of heaven to earth.

My openness and curiosity allowed new experiences to come into my life, in ways I never saw coming. My first book, "Light Me Up" will give specific examples, and so will Part II of this book, but they are more intimate. My daily disciplines helped me grow my muscle of awareness. That muscle is necessary to excavate the weeds of false identities and narratives that limitation is built on. I eventually moved beyond doubt and worry by tackling my fears to retrieve more love.

I am now on the other side of what seemed like an ocean that separated me from my authentic, true self. I found the pure love in me as priceless gold. When you feel it, you will know it too.

What I believe we all have in common is having bought into the image and program of limitation. To help lock us in we were taught to believe, "I only care about me, my family, my home, my money and my stuff." All of these beliefs created separation and a "service to self" ideology. We were turned against one another and became conditioned to believe war, rape, violence, lack and suffering were normal. We forgot our natural state of peace, purity, contentment and limitlessness. It's now time to remember.

It wasn't the propaganda of a virus that shook my world apart. It was a spiritual book that lit my inner spark and created a remembrance and a longing so deep that I was willing, committed and driven to do whatever it took to claim what was already mine - my sovereignty. My freedom wasn't found in someone having power over me. It was inside of me. Can you see my superhero cape now? Good! Because you have one too!

For me, the powerful spark that ignited when I read Yogananda's book was a feeling money could not buy because I had plenty of it, at that time. Like anything worthwhile in life, it required effort, focus and discipline to achieve the lasting results I knew were possible. That book gave me a sense of something different, and that different was magnetic and mind-altering. It was a force and it was inside of me. Nothing in life was more empowering than realizing my Higher Self was worthy of being trusted.

Religion had brainwashed me to see myself as unworthy. I mean no disrespect to your relationship with religion. For me, I had a strong attachment to suffering as a result of those teachings and my upbringing. When I could see more of the lies, there wasn't a switch that I could turn off to make it all go away. Instead, there were many steps I had to take in a new direction. My daily practices supported me in moving away from the old and toward something new.

My process returned me to my childhood over and over again to revisit things that were natural to me. Things I had learned to shame in myself. One of those was "knowing." I spoke about it earlier. When you know something, without knowing how you know it - you just know. That is heart clarity. It was normal for me as a child and I'm sure it was for you too. I thought it was common sense. I never doubted it. Until I learned from my caretakers that it was not good and therefore believed something was wrong with me.

I was highly aware of subtleties as a kid, which included feeling people's unexpressed emotions. Without emotional intelligence language I had no idea I was highly empathetic. I was an ultra-sensitive kid living in a world where nobody acknowledged their sixth sense. Yet it was the first language we all spoke in the womb. In short, my own family didn't accept the sensitive parts of me. That taught me to turn against my sensitivity too.

It wasn't until I read that book that I began to remember who I was. Then I needed to learn how to accept parts of myself that no one else could. What's the point of remembering who you are if kick those parts of yourself out again? That is why self-love is the greatest weapon you'll ever possess. It's like your inner human resource department where you make sure everyone is taken care of. You gotta love those parts of you to run more efficiently and get everyone on the payroll.

We all absorb life as infants and toddlers. It's called survival and the way we learn. We don't get to pick what sticks. The things we learn about life, love and ourselves when we are young, aren't always healthy for us. In fact, many of our thoughts and beliefs aren't worth repeating again. That's why it's important to gain sight of them.

I discovered there was more to life than what I was taught. Being a full-grown adult and realizing how emotionally and spiritually immature I was didn't feel good but I knew how to work hard and I kept at it. I got no results from my morning or evening meditations for months but I didn't stop. It was the first time in my life I wasn't working for someone else. I was working for my own liberation. Faith and trust were paychecks that came to alter my life.

I now experience the rewarding results of that one decision - to become my highest and greatest potential. I live with peace and satisfaction that money can't buy. I now feel the magnetism of my heart; a life force that lives and breathes as me.

Today, what I teach is what I live and what I have undergone. I understand the integration that the body undergoes in this transition. It can be shocking and disorienting to discover the lies when you grow your muscle of awareness. I know how much it hurts to lose people, jobs, homes, children and beliefs. And how rewarding it is to experience the limitlessness of my true nature.

It was tough to learn that I couldn't grip onto the heaven within me; while still holding onto the hell of suffering that defined me. Without the awareness that my heart brought me of my Higher Self, I would not have known I was feasting on a diet of pain and suffering, and not going for the gold. Funny thing is, by other people's standards, I was living a good life in that enslavement. Let me tell you, that was not living - that was surviving. I now know the difference.

My choice to step out of limitation was not unlike a decision to rise up the corporate ladder. My commitment required the same focus, discipline and training of obtaining an upper-level executive position, or going into the ring with the best fighter in the world. The only difference was I was choosing to climb the ladder of consciousness, and to battle my own demons.

Like going into the ring for the first time, I rarely saw the punches before impact because I was oblivious to my unconscious thoughts, habits and behaviors. My eyes were swollen, my head hung low, and my mind didn't know why it had to hurt so bad. But I stayed in the ring and came to see the swing before it could touch me. Eventually, each fist of fear lost its power to harm me because I went for the force behind its momentum, and found the golden gloves of love.

My decision to reach for the gold was worth all of the sweat, blood, tears of loss and blows to my head, because I am now well aware of my infinite spirit and know the power if it's punch. It lives in me in as my inner spark and authentic self. I feel wildly alive in my freedom to shine!

Chapter 10
Realized Wealth

I know you like wealth, but is it real? Why do you think men strive for financial success but don't hold the same value in becoming aware and balanced in mind, heart and body? I would conclude it is based on how society defined power. The images we were given around our bodies and our lives were based in limitation. Now that the power structures in society, and the identities around our bodies, hearts and minds are under reconstruction - it is time to redefine.

Think of Steve Jobs, who I am sure you respected. He put all of his energy into his work. I commend his ability to dream and imagine as he brought a spin on the word apple, and his invention invaded our world with revolutionary technology. Despite that, do you know what his thoughts were when he was dying? He posted the on social media. I'll share a portion of what he wrote below.

"I reached the pinnacle of success in the business world. In others' eyes, my life is an epitome of success. However, aside from work, I have little joy. In the end, wealth is only a fact of life that I am accustomed to. At this moment, lying on the sick bed and recalling my whole life, I realize that the recognition and wealth that I took so much pride in, have paled and become meaningless, in the face of impending death." -Steve Jobs, LinkedIn.

Gentlemen, our current definition of power didn't bring one of the greatest entrepreneurs of our time lasting happiness and satisfaction, when his life came to an end. He's not the only one who died with regrets. The five most common regrets of the dying are:

1) I wish I hadn't worked so hard. 2) I wish I dared to live a life true to myself, not the life others expected of me. 3) I wish I dared to express my feelings. 4) I wish I had stayed in touch with my friends. 5) I wish I had let myself be happier. (Bronnie Ware; Top Five Regrets of the Dying).

Money isn't who you are gentlemen. If you are awesome at making it, good for you! That's great! I'm proud of you. But there's more to life and I don't want you to miss out. I am suggesting you put your money where your infinite spirit is and set your goal on "realized" wealth. You invest in you, and that investment impacts the collective, your business, your family and all who have the privilege of passing through your life.

The challenging part of personal growth is that you need to hold yourself accountable to your investment - in you. No one will be sending you monthly profit and loss statements; indicating your losses when you: skip your exercises, don't listen to your gut instincts and miss phenomenal opportunities at the expense of burning your steak. There will be no print out of your unhealthy food choices, alcohol or drug consumption. Nobody will be calling you to their office to discuss the argument and unhappy situations that remain in your life because you won't face your fears to get to the other side. Those major losses will not be on any fancy card stock with Higher Kingdom letterhead on top for you to review each month. You are the one who has to keep you in-check.

You can hire me for backup support and I will be a phone call away. But it is you I am employing to be the CEO of your life. As for your profits, you'll clearly see and sense those rewards the more you depend on your Higher Self to guide you. I certainly don't want to see you back at the grill burning that expensive filet.

The new model of man embodies "realized" wealth. His new higher standard shows in the way he carries himself. He employs his inner authority and chooses to mature with his Higher Self by his side. Living life from the inside out - is life of the highest standard. When you are dialed in like this, you will not slide into home base at the end of your life with regrets. All of your eggs won't be in one basket. You will have diversified and invested in the most important relationship of your life.

"Realized" wealth doesn't just fall into your lap. You must want it and work for it. Your awakening is an inside job, done by you and supported by people like me. I'm just putting the kingdom in front of you. It is you who must choose to reach for it each day.

There is a shift that takes place when you go for realized wealth. Developing physical and emotional maturity is a spiritual experience and it brings balance. It will be uncomfortable at times, just like the market going up and down. You will learn to adapt to not having to understand, or having to like it, as the process of surrender into the quantum field of intelligence within you, is a little awkward at first because it involves trusting your operating system. Like learning things backwards, this is the opposite of control. The very part of you that you learned to mistrust, you must now befriend. The process of "allowing" your inner authority to guide you becomes easier when you let the habits and beliefs that are stopping you - fall away.

Remember, we've been in the dark about a lot of things for quite some time. That darkness is just lack of information. When you open to more possibilities, you step out of that darkness and into the light of pure potential. There's more to receive and it's why you want to remain open, curious and intentional. We are going from conditional ways and conditional love to becoming unconditional to ourselves.

To get a sense of what that may feel like think about linear versus round. It's not just one straight line, there's a flow to life that many don't experience because they are busy controlling every aspect through their own unseen fears. Instead of trusting themselves and life they bear down and stop the natural flow of receiving. Many of these natural aspects of who we are, such as: sensing, receiving and feeling are feminine qualities, that have been ignorantly portrayed as weak. Nothing could be farther from the truth. These aspects are in us all, regardless of our gender, and they are quite superior. It's time we respect them as the higher intelligence that communicates to and through us.

We'll end this chapter by taking you back to the womb once again to sense and perceive more. How did you survive in the womb? You were the essence of purity and surrender. All that you needed was given to you. You weren't designed to suffer or to be in want of anything. Receiving all that you needed was natural and you surrendered to the unconditional love and support that nurtured and designed you. I've seen grown men know how to surrender at the time of orgasm, so you do remember how this works. The warmth of comfort, connection and even ecstasy are found in the act of surrender. There's nothing weak about it. Surrender is a foundational component to our existence. And, it brings good things.

In the womb, we got what we needed because life takes care of us. That is worth remembering. We were designed to live in harmony and that is what "realized" wealth is about. It's about an appreciation and a happiness that is ours to claim. This new way of life is about our alignment with our True Self. Instead of reaching for things that you believe you lack, perceive and believe you are; respected, guided, and abundantly provided for every day and every way. Allow life to come to you, just like you did when you were in the womb, and then you will see.

Chapter 11
Getting Out of the Bunker

Golfing and growing a tree both take time. The radical transformation I underwent was an integration of my mind, body and heart. That was a realization of my spirit in human form. And I'm still transforming as limitlessness has no end. The new human we are becoming requires a balance by listening to more than just our minds. In this digital age, many have missed the mark by reaching for instant gratification, which does not challenge the human spirit to grow. It takes time to liberate ourselves.

To begin living as my highest and greatest potential, I employed more rigid exercises than I am teaching you because I know that you have the advantage of all the work that's already been done. All you need to do is to carve out the fifteen minutes each morning and you'll connect into a wave of change that's already here. I'm preparing your mind and prepping your body for the change that is at hand.

My new habits included meditation, eating healthier, turning off the television, spending more time in nature, being choosy about the company I kept, and everything I put into my mind and body. Preservatives in foods, and in soaps and shampoos were eliminated. Fluoride, food colorings, corn syrup and all harmful ingredients no longer were permitted to enter my system. It was like tending a garden, learning to manage my mind and body with more awareness.

I had to see the weeds of limiting thoughts and harmful ingredients that were free to flourish before I knew better. Beliefs like "only this way works and nothing else is possible" had to go. Thoughts that convinced me that I was a good woman for trying to make everyone else happy and that it was my obligation, had to go. People-pleasers are sacrificing themselves like martyrs for no one's benefit. I was one of them but not anymore.

Sadly, those behaviors teach our kids terrible habits like; giving our power over to another is normal and expected. It also portrays that power is dangerous and best to be given away. That doesn't teach healthy boundaries. It teaches kids how to not honor themselves. When we have no awareness around our own needs, we don't have firm boundaries. When we don't honor ourselves, we rarely practice self-care. There's no self-love or Higher Self in that way of living. It's learned limited behavior.

The reason we use a small percent of our potential is because we are stuck in patterns or unhealthy cycles. I gave you the visual of the locomotive headed back to the station where it started in a loop. The way to get out of the loop/pattern is to develop the witness or observer in you. The wise man who can see your life from a bird's eye view. Time in nature, exercise, journaling, mediation, massage, baths, and yoga are practices that support my habit of reflection which strengthens the witness in me. A variety of new books and spiritual teachings, as well as, working with different professionals and coaches in the healing arts, opened me up to new thoughts and possibilities.

Regular body work also became a part of my self-care regimen. When I speak about my spirit becoming embodied, that means my presence shows up in my body. I came to notice different areas of my body just by breathing and tuning into it more. I was smart enough to know that I could not achieve different results by doing the same things I had been doing, and that's why I gave you exercises that will force you into a new habit if you don't allow your stubbornness to stop you from employing them. I employed new healthy habits, that are still a part of my life today. That is how I steered my unconscious locomotive out of the loop and onto the track of limitlessness.

I had to also learn not to judge the process. Personal mastery will be unique to each of you. Just like your golf game. It's your own swing, clubs and mindset that govern your game. You know when you grab your driver to tee off, and you eye-up the flag far away? Think of personal mastery like that; keeping your eye on the goal (of becoming your highest and greatest potential) and then giving it your best swing, each and every day. While surrendering to where the ball lands. That's how it works.

You can't take the next swing until you get to where the ball landed. It's a whole new game again from that new position. There may be something to heal at that next juncture. It requires a different club, perhaps the deep breathing club. And then observation of the feelings that arise may inform you that your assumption of the pitching wedge is now not the best choice, because you tuned into the feelings that gave you more information than your assumption. Maybe you never took time to consider a different angle but your breathing opened you up to trying something new. Breath is key, as is the understanding that this work is a process of - one step at a time. Just like golf.

Society may not talk about the importance of facing traumas and emotions as being normal, healthy, and a natural process of human growth - but it is. Not unlike a tree growing from a seed. It has to break out of a shell, dig its roots into the dark, cold earth before even seeing the light of day. Above the surface, it becomes a very different version of itself; one limb and one leaf at a time. We are very much like that when we move out of our patterns. We break out of a mold and grow. Parts of us die away for new parts to come forth. The parts that die can hurt and we grieve their loss but we don't stop growing. Many of you have stopped growing and that needs to change. I want my lions to go all the way with me.

You may walk down the links and find your ball landed in a bunker but that doesn't mean you stop playing the game. You just need to dig deeper. Use a new club (new habit) and give it a swing that gets it up and out of the drama. By taking the lessons and ending the unhealthy cycle. You have to be willing to clear out the emotions that were buried like that ball in the sand. You don't just walk away from the ball because it landed in the sand. You go into the bunker prepared to work things out. I need you to do the same with your emotional body.

Reconciliation is another important step along the links of life. Each time you make peace with the past: by letting go of attachment to people, situations, habits and beliefs where you were wronged; denied your own feelings, or hurt someone else because you could. There is a process of reconciliation that is important. We may feel awful and need to cry or punch a pillow, take a boxing class, or talk to someone who can listen to our thoughts and feelings. All are important to do because it brings you to a new level of awareness. Each time we heal and reconcile we move to another level of peace and satisfaction - on the other side. Like the perfect swing out of the bunker. It brings us new possibilities that are far better than when we were stuck.

Same goes for a tree. Growth is a process and although trees deal with mold, insects, and fire that threaten its health and well-being. We deal with traumas from unconscious people and outdated beliefs, corrupt influences, and personal agendas that structure our thinking. Healing is to be respected. It is a natural process we all go through to grow and evolve.

We've been on an old operating system. Built by old thought forms rooted in the belief of pain and suffering. We were taught limitation and to believe in illness and disease. What happens when you believe in your limitless nature? Could you go grow young? If you could believe in limitation could you believe in the opposite?

Getting the heart embodied (in the body) to share in the process with the mind requires using more of your operating system. To handle the tight curves in my high-performance vehicle, I had to confront inherited and conditioned belief systems that caused me to doubt myself. I wanted to hold onto limitation because I believed it kept me safe.

It's normal to find yourself unsteady in your new vehicle as old emotions, memories and beliefs surface. It was disorienting for me at times. I'm here to let you know it's okay to feel sensitive as the old programs are identified for removal. They'll fall away on their own. You only need to gain sight of them. It's actually your sensitivity that works as a radar system to discover areas that need more of your attention.

At times, becoming more aware was like waking up to discover my entire garden was full of weeds. Depending on how focused you are, you may see a bunch all at once. That could propel a concentrated period of reconciliation where you need to be extra patient with yourself, while your heart and mind make peace with the past. Other weeds may take more time because the root structures are so embedded.

Do your best to release your judgments and expectations around emotions and the weeds you see that need to go. Removing weeds can be a dirty job so remember to ask for help when you need it. Be curious and observe the sensations in your body as you move through your process. Like eyeing your ball from all angels see where you are restricted in your body. Breathe into those places. If you get to discover you are holding back and containing yourself to compartmentalize your feelings, observe that. This is about having a closer relationship with your body and becoming aware of your energy. It's not about fleeing the present moment to distract yourself. That is the old program.

When you start to catch onto your unconscious habits, try not to deflect or to get down on yourself. Notice the habit, bring in breath and be your best friend by not abandoning you. Your feelings matter. This is how we weave self-love and awareness into the bunkers within us that once kept us stuck. If you want your full operating system on-line, you must be willing to go into the trap, with your club of awareness and take a few swings to get yourself out.

We all mastered stuffing our emotions because we were taught - they were unacceptable. I'm sorry we were all misinformed. Emotions are not who we are; they are temporary fields of frequency informing us. If you find yourself in a bunker and the sand feels like it's taking you deeper - remember to breathe. Ask the wise man, your Higher Self to help you. Be open to receiving a new level of freedom, from the place you are currently stuck. There's a lesson to take forward when you stay with the feeling and let that information inform you. Don't just whack at the discomfort, like you are beating it to death. Feel into your body, use your compassionate touch and allow the dynamic intelligence of your heart to inform you through your body.

Ask yourself, where is their pain or sensation in your body? Presence entering areas of your body that were once shut off requires the explorer in you to be curious. That is an area where presence can now inhabit, when you choose the club of awareness to heal the ball (of past pain) that is stuck there. Consider it your inner bunker and now you know where to put your attention. That ball may have landed there when you were a little boy. Now the grown man in you can take the time to help the pain be free by grabbing the club of patients and love that the little boy never got. He was stuck in that bunker and needed you to help him out.

When you discover where in your body you are feeling the sensation, aid that part of yourself by breathing into that place, or by putting your hand there and silently saying to that part of yourself, "It's okay, I am here. You are safe." Bring comfort in the form of healing to parts of yourself that needed that care and attention and never got it. Don't overthink it. Just give yourself the respect of healing. It works. Trust me. You'll be wiser, lighter, happier and freer as a result.

Curiosity and conscious breathing will help you choose the right club and precise swing, each and every time. If you are meant to land in a bunker, it's not bad luck. It's an opportunity to get yourself unstuck from something in your life that's been buried in your body. When you ignore what's been buried it can become a health issue after it's tried to work itself out in relationship dynamics.

When you find yourself up and out of the bunker, with more compassion in your heart knowing the trap didn't swallow you up, perhaps you'll see how well you freed yourself. The bunker had a treasure for you. When you stayed in the discomfort and followed the feeling you got to the core. Presence is what breath will bring us.

The next time you are stuck and don't see a way out - remember to breathe. That's an invitation to your Higher Self, as your club of awareness, to help you out of any bunker. We want to remember that club because there are parts of us that have been stuck and may now be buried so far down, we can't see them. But by tuning into our body signals we can sense them. We have what it takes to get them unstuck. Your club of awareness will show you where they are buried. The power of your heart will free them.

Nice game gentlemen. Please hit the showers and meet me in the dark.

Chapter 12
Come into the Dark with Me

It's light in here. Welcome to the unknown. This is the place where many are afraid to come. The place that exists beyond certainty that is limitless. It's not as scary as you think. In fact, it's quite spacious and supportive but you've got to come in here with me, to know what I am telling you is true. Yes, it's unknown. But it's not here to hurt you. Imagine it as the womb which was also a dark and mysterious place.

We were all conceived in the unknown. All alone inside our mother we surrendered into form. Nine months later we were birthed into another unknown. In other words, the unknown is more familiar than we allow ourselves to remember. It's more natural than we think. It was a place that alchemized our purity into human form.

You learned just like I did; to believe only what the eyes could see. That thinking shut us off from remembering to sense and perceive. Our human potential was squeezed into limited beliefs and images. What got buried and hidden in limitation was the power of the heart to sense and to know. I believe the unknown is housed in the heart. And to get to know it better we must accept the feminine aspects of who we are, as we were designed in a female body. The ability to sense is innate in all of us whether we have breasts and ovaries, or not.

This is not about making a man into a woman. I love men. I'm a champion for men. This is about balance and our greatest potential. This is about us being the best players at the game of life by tapping into our limitless nature by incorporating more of who we are. The unknown is a place I'd like you to get comfortable with because the seen and the unseen are natural parts of who we are.

The innocence that formed us never goes away, even if we built a fortress of protection around it. It's still in us. And it's our job to nurture that part of ourselves. When we don't, we become rigid, cold, disconnected and mentally overdeveloped, operating more like computers than humans with heart. Parts of our bodies get ignored when we remain absorbed in our minds.

Let's return to nurturing to better understand the unknown. We all needed our mothers to nurture us but why didn't we pick up where she left off? A part of us will always appreciate being nurtured as our softness is still inside of us. Would you say no to a light touch all over your skin because it felt too good? I doubt it. To nurture is to allow softness, the purity of our innocence, to be physically felt. It's not something to intellectualize but we can feel its existence within us. That is touching into the unknown.

The aspects of our feminine nature have been denied and controlled. We all learned to bury our softness to survive. As a result, we created a cold, cruel world where war, rape and violence exist as normalcy. That may seem like it's out "in the world" but actually every single day people are in their own inner battle. What is seen on the outside is a projection of what is happening on the inside. That is why I suggest gaining sight of your thoughts.

The huge problems we are addressing in our world stems from ignoring what is in our hearts. When our mind is too busy distracting us we can't hear our hearts and pay attention to our body signals. I am asking each and every one of you to raise your standards and become the solution. As the old control system crumbles, we have an opportunity to take independent responsibility to gain sight of unhealthy characteristics within us and around us, in order to create change.

Once we gain sight, we open the doorway to the unknown. That place of creation houses our limitless potential. It is a place of safety. That is where we activate the dormant and unrealized parts ourselves. The unknown allows us the opportunity for the new version of ourselves to take form. Think of it as going back to the mother to transform ourselves, and to remember our original design. Imagine that mother any way you wish. Her womb of the unknown is a place of safety. Although it's dark and you don't know what you'll look like on the other side, it's safe to enter. You are loved and held.

When life is truly valued and honored, innocence and the need to nurture humans will be upheld by the community. Remedies won't be forced on a population, conveying they are helpless and limited. People will remember to obey the force of nature within them. They will realize the unknown as a part of who they are.

To feel again is to remember that sensing life through your body is natural and normal. Your intuition or gut instincts are the guidance system of your inner authority that speaks without words, and doesn't have to wait for your rational mind to believe or to even understand. It's not only natural it is like nature itself.

116

It's the part of you that just knows and makes no apologies for that knowing. That is what exists in the unknown.

We do not have to physically die and come back as an infant to transform. I've done this enough times to know that we rebirth ourselves as we evolve, regardless of our gender. We go into the unknown of our limitless nature where new possibilities exist. We try on new things as ways of being. We transform as adults just as we did as children who remembered to dream. Evolution is a natural part of our experience as an infinite being. That is why I give you the image of the womb and my unconditional love to hold you through this important process of personal growth. Our change is natural.

If you want to keep this in your mind, let me introduce you to your right brain, which wouldn't be in your head if you didn't need it. Invite the explorer back into your life and tap into your imagination. Let your heart remind you how you feel when something lights you up. Open to your creativity and imagine designing a new you. Dream a little. Ask yourself, if your body could do anything what would it do? Expand your mind into your limitless potential by dreaming.

Consider the unknown; a safe place to make the transition from certainty (same old) to something new (uncertain & limitless). How do you dream a new you into form? Think about how you express your creativity and how you could express it more. What gets you excited? What are you passionate about? What inspires you?

It's time for some homework. Tonight, or this weekend, I want you to sit down and write a list of all the things that inspire you. Think back to being a kid again. What did you enjoy doing? If the kid in you could do anything with your body, what would he do? If you could do anything with your life from this moment forward, what would you do?

I certainly didn't dream big enough at the start of my change. It was only after my bravery of going into the unknown over and over again, that I brought forth a kingdom. The unknown is where I sculpted a new me and remembered my innocence that knew how to dream. In the unknown, I felt into the wild nature within me. What came forth over time was a sensual, unrestrained expression as me.

You could say I learned to take one step at a time just like an infant but as a full-grown adult. Since we don't take evolution classes to know that this is normal, I had to learn on my own. What I was in the process of doing was simply embracing my own expression of pure love. I'm still in the process but I had no idea that purity could take form in the ways it has in me.

Now you know, evolving is just like birth. It's a normal process and it's okay to be anxious or nervous but you don't want to stop the birth by letting your fears control you. Learn to let go of the resistance by going into the fear. Allow yourself to land in that warm, dark space of the unknown to be held and nurtured, and birthed into something new. It is the safest place you can find yourself. Get used to it because you return to the unknown again and again. Each time an old belief, job, relationship, image or habit falls away, there is an opportunity to move into the unknown limitless nature of your unrealized potential and form into something new.

Chapter 13
Everyone Wins

And the entire game is in your hands. There's a quantum field of potential within you that exists as the new reality for men who choose to accept and lead with heart. Who you are is a certain type of creativity based on that Spark within you. These are the new leaders of today and tomorrow who can take things further based on their joy and life experience. When you give yourself permission to stand apart from the things that limit you. These are the men that will no longer choose to live unconsciously through habit, or for the sake of fitting in, to land the deal, to score the woman, or to take advantage of any situation, person, or opportunity for personal gain at the harm of another.

Service to self and limitation is the old program. The higher standard of performance, which begins with a relationship with your inner spark or Higher Self is about a new level of accountability, exclusive to the men who rise and become the new model of man, aligned in his highest and greatest potential. He cares about his well-being and service to others.

There are new possibilities that exist here. Things we've never even seen or experienced before become realized. We can accomplish more when it's natural to move toward collaborative leadership, as ruling over people is disempowering, controlling and dominating. Shared power will become normal. We will become the superior technology and together we will generate more innovative products and services as our individual creativity expands and expresses itself.

In a supportive work environment where each individual contributes to the whole - it's okay to be different. When our enlightened state is brought into the equation as a normal part of existence, the human potential expands. When we bring the best of us into our life, we naturally bring that out in others. It is seen and felt in the work that we do. Everyone thrives and we learn and grow together.

When the owner and leader of the business is free from the programs of the past he gives and receives in a whole new way. There is a wealth consciousness realized in our highest and greatest potential that isn't a solitary reflection of a bank account but an embodied state of being. The aware and awakened man who designed the company emanates his success and money follows him. He attracts through his magnetism motored by his heart.

Heart and mind working together eliminates programs of lack that impeded the natural flow of abundance that is available. The need to dominate no longer exist in his workplace to limit growth or to intimidate employees. He understands an entire workforce makes the business profitable and his fears of miserliness can fall away.

Women are welcomed into more leadership roles as an example of how feelings in the workplace can create unity; a sense of togetherness that fuels the success of the entire company. If it takes men a while to learn how to feel again, women can be a guiding influence in what it means to nurture your business, as you would a child. Aware men are not ashamed of their personal development and welcome the support. Just as women welcome and appreciate what men can teach them about business and finance. The time has come where mutual respect goes both ways. We accept that we need each other in a mindset of service to others. Just as we need the right and left hemispheres of our brain.

As new leaders in our world we become guardians of a loving existence. Men no longer want to take from women but instead they want to give them more opportunities. Women thrive in a supportive workforce and establish more financial independence. She can use her developed senses to bring about new solutions that weren't welcomed in the former structure, where she was expected to be more like a man to fit-in.

Businesses with heart may support family-life, exercise and time for creative endeavors. These simple yet important factors of life can be seen as essentials to people flourishing. The welfare of the planet will be important in how business operates as service to others includes caring for the planet. The bottom line will include emotional and spiritual wellbeing and not just a balance sheet of dollar signs. The whole of the human will be factored in when heart hits home.

Our personal development directly impacts our entire business and all who work with us. When there's a sense of nurture and a shared prosperity woven into the fabric of what we do it shows in a collective performance and in a spirit of joy. When people feel nurtured and taken care of, they thrive. That "something special" feeling that comes from your company makes others want to replicate your innovative success. You took business to heart and it changed the way business was done.

The same qualities that build a business can build you. Life isn't meant to happen only after you come home from work. The joy of life is meant to be lived in every moment. That's why you want to heal the past, create a new you and live in your greatest potential. Our natural passions and specialties are to be realized and infused into the work that we do, every day. When we live with purpose, we give up regrets. We enjoy life. When we use our courage to merge feeling and logic, we risk living life to the fullest. We have no idea what's possible when we raise the standard of our own performance, by incorporating the whole of what makes us human. When we learn to live life from the inside out, everyone wins.

Conclusion of Part I

We face challenges and overcome obstacles as a process of growth. Pain doesn't go away because we grow more aware of our infinite potential but more solutions do arise. As the old thought forms and characteristic traits that no longer serve us are laid to rest. The only way we will stop stepping on the hearts of humanity is by learning to embrace our own. Our limitless nature is waiting for us to take part in creation.

This isn't about a political side or religious dogma; this is about personal mastery that makes you the leader of your own life from the inside out. As you can see, I lead leaders to their own wisdom and I cheer on their highest and greatest potential.

The value of human existence is what is at hand and it's ready to be upgraded exponentially. You don't achieve different results by doing things the same way. That is why I have given you simple, practical exercises and have introduced you to your other half. The part of you that can see more; a muscle that builds every time you gain sight. When you let go of the beliefs and habits of the past, you have the opportunity to walk into the unknown.

My seduction is about living life of the highest standard. It's your own independent responsibility and daily commitment to design your life from the inside out. Only you can tap into the invincible power of your heart. We no longer have the luxury of pointing fingers and thinking that changes anything. We must be the solution to bring about a balance of mind and heart.

By waking up to the power within my heart it inspired me to reach out to you. I am willing to grow into my infinite spirit and to become my highest and greatest potential, and be surrounded by millions of lions (in the form of awakening men) who join me.

Now that I am in your life, no matter what you lose and let go of, my love, respect and belief in you remains. It is safe to grow and change. It's safe to see yourself as limitless and to embrace the spirit in your heart that is here to shine! Be the infinite spark of who you are by breaking out of limitation. Personal growth is for the warrior in you. When you let old images fall away and learn to unconditionally love yourself, you will understand the heart of who you are is - a Higher Kingdom. I am here to inspire you to claim what's rightfully yours.

Chapter 14
Ladies Please Join Me

Please give me a moment to say goodbye to the men. Good work guys! I'm proud of you for taking the time to let me blow your mind a little. I hope you took good notes and are willing to die to the old. And become more wildly alive than ever. Before we move on, let me honor your brilliant and cuddle your compassionate heart. Please close your eyes and feel the heat of my breath as I lean closer to you, stroking that large… mane of yours and nuzzling your neck. My lips softly kiss your cheek and I whisper these last words to you, "I believe in you."

This next section is for the ladies. Please go ahead and hold the door open for them. Hello, and welcome Ladies! I will show you what I discovered hidden in the dark shadows of my own ignorance. Body and sexual shame were hidden so well, I didn't even know how resistant I was to my own pleasure. I had been programmed as a toddler that my feminine flower was bad. Society, religion and my upbringing also taught me that sex was bad. Being naive and trusting, I took in those teachings of repression. That resulted in limiting my body, mind and heart from being connected.

To heal these particular fears, I had to gain sight of mixed-up messages that were planted in my mind as a little girl. I had been programed to believe that the goal in life for a female was to marry and become a wife and mother. Organized religion layered on the belief that my body was to remain virginal and was meant for "one man only." In other words, someone outside of me was the boss and authority of my body. I had to do what I was instructed. I was to give my body and life to a man. Family, society and religion taught me to give my power and pleasure away, making me believe they weren't for me.

At the start of Part II, that "one man" was now my x-husband. The end of our marriage was very difficult for me. You can read about that in my first book, "Light Me Up" where I share more details about mysterious changes, encounters and travels that took place over that long and painful year of divorce. Once my marriage was over, I was in the position of facing new fears that weren't accessible while married. My behaviors in marriage were bound to codependency, being the "good girl," people-pleaser. Guilt and shame kept me in check by controlling my body, mind and heart.

Although this next section may sound like a romance novel inwardly it was painful to walk through my fears. Being obedient to the laws placed on me was the only reality I knew, until I challenged those beliefs by gaining sight of them through new experiences. The rewards of going into the dark to realize the light in me; changed me as a woman. That took time and a variety of experiences before I made peace with sex and claimed my sensual nature. It was also a revelation to discover my body as a spiritual vessel of wisdom. No one had ever told me the psychical was spiritual but now I know.

All of the loss that came before me crossing the bridge to face my sexual fears was so great, I didn't know I had it in me to rise up. In Part II I strip it all. I invite you to get a little hot and bothered with me as I share my evocative experience of becoming sensually awakened through the touch of my skin; in union with men from various backgrounds and ethnicities all around the world. It wasn't easy to face sexual and body shame, over and over again. But every time I did, it was like the shield maiden in me battling for her own freedom.

Every time I got to strip more of my own fears, limited beliefs and baggage I embodied the freedom in my heart, felt through my skin. Falling in love with my sacred body and slaying the lies that controlled its natural needs and connection to my spirit, is why you will see me stepping out on stage in a full body black catsuit, to celebrate every curve that defines my form. This section is not a classroom, it is my stage where I bare all. Adults only.

For the men who choose to read this section, it will make you more aware of how you influence what women learn about themselves, by the way you respect her body. For the men who do take a seat in this audience... beware. I cover a lot of territory both geographically and figuratively. It's written for women and includes far more details that matter to us. Consider this section an adult field trip from the classroom. Pack your snacks. This is a voyage. If you choose to come along or not, be sure to meet me back for a taste of Sex & Balances.

Ladies, shall we?

PART II: The Men

The 12 years I spent with the same man were over. I was in shock as my heart shattered into a million pieces. After moving through some of the grief from the loss of: the people I loved, our beautiful home together, my work, friends, neighbors and my life as I knew it; I was encouraged to date again. It would have taken me even longer to sleep with another man after my marriage, had the first man not been such a fiery, aggressive alpha. He was (and still is) a very handsome, smart, confident, dark-haired Italian man. When the Italian Stallion galloped into my life, I had no idea I had so much to learn about my own body.

We met on a dating site while I was still living back east and before I had any idea I would be moving west. This man was charming, sexy, and as self-assured as they come. He was polite and respectful on our first date, taking me to dinner and charming me with his clever mind and handsome presence. By the third date, his playful flirting increased substantially. His dark eyes, dark hair, intelligent wit and mischievous grin pulled me in. But there was no chance I would ever sleep with him. So I thought.

I had decades of idealistic thinking that shamed me into a corner and didn't allow my body to know pleasure. The rules and restrictions included the "one man," who would have to marry me, would have more rights to my body than I did. How do you break free of slut-shaming and guilt to enjoy your body and spiritual nature as a woman? Well, that was a process.

When you live a life controlled by outer authority, you learn to stop listening to your own body's instincts and needs. I was in a complete disconnect with my own body. I was trained from childhood that my body was bad and others were the boss of it. That was my situation, and this section will show you how my unexpected progression was an education and a physical and spiritual embodiment, that I never saw coming. It took one heroic step after the next to see my programming and habits in order for anything to change. But before I go there, I'm going to give you a brief history about me. It will help to give you an idea of how far I came. In case you didn't read my first book, "Light Me Up" this will give you a snapshot.

I grew up in blue collar town and came from a lineage of housewives, representative of a lifestyle I didn't initially embrace myself. Instead, I went to college and obtained a corporate sales job. I made more money per year than my father, by the time I was 25. The man I would come to meet at my dream job and later marry, would force me to abort our child, push me out of my dream job and eventually suggest part-time work for me, to be more available in my role as step-mother. That is a lot of information. I can't breeze over it without expressing the pain of never wanting to give up my child. But he was a big executive and insisted I had no other choice. I believed him because I was in the habit of doing as I was told, and always believing everything was my fault. That is because I was well trained as a child who lived the terror of what a man in charge can do, to those he controls.

I learned to sacrifice my body and heart without knowing it. Thanks to my conditioning, I was taught other people's needs, beliefs and opinions were important, not mine. Codependency wasn't a choice; it was a way of life. A way I would need to unlearn as a conscious adult. But not in a marriage that replicated the same submissive codependency I had known in my youth. None of this information is pretty but to better understand the layers of guilt, victimhood and shame I was buried beneath, it helps you understand what I was overcoming in these sexual encounters to come.

It's even difficult for me to look back and see how weak, frightened and controlled I was when I didn't have clear sight of myself. If I had been the woman I am today there's not a chance I would have given up my child or the job I loved. But sadly, I was controlled and programmed by the belief that people had power over me. I feel for the woman I once was who was left to mourn the pain of such great loss alone. The shame I felt by how he reacted to my pregnancy was as painful as the procedure. The loss was even worse. It hurt my body and it broke my heart. My childhood had groomed me to face physical pain and to believe it was my fault and that I deserved it. Even when there was no evidence whatsoever that I did anything wrong. In this case, I was again taking blame and being obedient to the dictates of someone outside of me being the boss. I ignorantly did not think I had a choice.

Years later, at the end of our marriage, he would remove the only other child I would come to mother and then make it impossible for me to ever see her again. As painful as that was, it wasn't even the full extent of my loss, there was much more. In summary, I'll just say, I had very little will to live. All that I loved was gone. They say grieving is when love has no place to go. That was exactly where I was and on my own.

With all of that said, you may now understand why I felt like I had been tragically rear-ended and thrown out the windshield when my marriage came to a plot-thickening end. I was forced to piece myself back together, in a whole new way. The scrapes and shards of glass would metaphorically appear in my wounded heart that would take me years to repair. By doing the necessary healing work of my own personal growth, I rose up and out of my "western dream" that crashed and killed the facade that was me.

What life had to teach me after it was all stripped away; were things I never knew, would never have chosen, and would never have seen or believed. My first book covers many strange and unexplained experiences that opened me up to the unseen worlds within me. However, this book shares simplified teachings of the unseen world, and escorts you into the dark and, "said to be," forbidden realms of sexuality; to show you what I claimed for myself in the darkness, one man, and one realization at a time. This section is where I embrace the dark and make no apologies for my light. Come and meet "The Men."

Chapter 15
The Italian Stallion

Needless to say, a year plus after the crash I wasn't very open but the Italian Stallion was the perfect force of nature, to push me to face more fears to feel again. Each time I went on a date with the Stallion, I dodged his advances, until I could no longer.

One night, as he was dropping me off from our date he asked if he could use the bathroom and have a drink of water before he drove home. I had not planned on inviting him in but agreed to his request, pointed him to the bathroom, and waited in the kitchen with his water. He gulped it down, slammed the glass on the low counter, leaned up against me, and gave me a wet kiss. This man could breathe smoke out of his nose like a dragon in the way he burned with passion.

Like a magician, he swept me up onto the counter and waived his wand like fingers and swoosh, my panties were off. I was nervous and excited as my defenses had no time to prepare for his sexual hunger. As an onlooker, I'm sure it was a hot "50 shades of gray" scene with two sexy bodies grinding on a smooth, black sheet of granite. He moved so quickly I didn't see the condom go on but I did feel his steel-hard cock fight its way into me. My mind was screaming, "Stop!" but my body had already been invaded by a man on a mission. He wanted nothing more than to be inside of me and he accomplished that with some serious force.

My body wasn't ready and I'm not shaming him but I am pointing out that today, I appreciate and value consensual sex with a man who knows more about me and my body, before he enters what I consider my sacred center. The Stallion was the first man who began to bring my body and sexual shame to my attention. I was in the difficult process of becoming an empowered woman, and this very intimate area of growth was brand new to me. My feminine body parts wanted to make themselves more known to me, and they did that night. I had to listen because I had not felt that much pain there since the surgery. I was too busy going through the motions of serving my husband to ever realize I had needs too.

The beginning of my "spiritual awakening" had only begun a few years prior. I was in the process of developing my muscle of awareness and had made many changes in my life but not between my thighs. My marriage had not permitted growth in this intimate area; therefore, I had no idea how disconnected I was from my own body, and its pleasure.

To be flung into overcoming sexual shame, after carrying a heavy heart of grief around, was its own swift learning curve, that played out over time. It's much easier to analyze all these years later as I reflect. It's also worth sharing because it may help you find compassion in your hearts for the women in your lives, and it may also teach you valuable aspects about life, and the wisdom and needs of our body.

One of those valuable aspects about life are boundaries. My parents didn't teach me about my own value or needs. Since I didn't place value on myself, I didn't acknowledge that I had needs. Therefore, I didn't know how to establish boundaries. I believe all 3 go hand-in-hand; valuing ourself, understanding our needs and setting boundaries. Raised in codependency through family teachings and religion, I was brainwashed to believe females were subservient to men. That we weren't equals. And, as I stated earlier those teachings conveyed my body was meant for his pleasure, not my own. Those beliefs established patterns that supported someone outside of me controlled my body. Although I was 35 years old, and had been sexually active with my former husband, I had very little knowledge about my own body and its pleasure. It was about his wants and needs while we were together. I believe many women have fallen into a similar trap.

I am all for hot, passionate and spontaneous sex in the kitchen that the Stallion facilitated, but I was still operating in the old belief and habit of sex being about the man. The pain I felt when he entered me was a wake-up call to listen to my body and to get know it better. I was not aware of its needs when I was going through the motions of sex with my husband, but this new man forced me to become more aware.

We never know what we are missing until we have tasted it. In this case, I had to first feel pain before I found pleasure. That's the gift that new situations and environments bring. They promote change and possibility, while pushing us out of habit. Nothing had changed in the sex department while I was married because I was living out "relationship rules" that were taught to me. It didn't require my free thinking and physical embodiment. I was enslaved by patterns that weren't about my joy, empowerment or pleasure, but rather my role.

Without the knowledge and wisdom of my heart and body that I possess today. I was merely an instrument of someone else's pleasure and not an embodied participant. Those 12 years prior to the Stallion the man I was with never took the time to help me to get to know my body. I didn't even realize I had gone that long satisfying someone else's needs, without ever once having an orgasm myself.

The spiritual book that woke me up, to choosing to become my highest and greatest potential created a lot of change in the last 2 years of my marriage. I had developed my daily meditation practices that fueled self-inquiry. Those practices combined with my weekly therapy sessions, allowed me to address my childhood abuse and codependency issues. My deep healing had begun and the process was now taking me to a new level, and into a new area of self-realization. One that required physical experiences, in order for me to embody my power/spirit in areas of my body that were not yet realized.

The changes I was making while married pushed my husband's buttons because he liked the woman who didn't question anything and who didn't know differently. My growing awareness challenged him, and I became the person to blame for all of his unresolved emotions and feelings that started to surface. Everything became my fault. That's another thing that can happen when one person is raring to grow, and the other is resistant to change. How he connived the end was not pretty, kind or in the least bit loving and considerate.

Now out of my marriage, I had the opportunity to face and heal more shame and unworthiness in areas of my body that I had learned to repress. The pain I felt when the first new cock entered my body could not be ignored. My body wasn't wet and ready to be entered. I had not even known what sex was like without artificial lubricant. That wasn't something used when the Stallion entered me because he was rearing to go. And there was no conversation prior to sex. Still being inhibited, I didn't say anything, nor did I know at that time how naturally wet my body could get prior to intercourse to let him know I needed more time. That was because no man had ever taken the time to pleasure and adore me first, for me to know how delightful I could feel from the inside out.

I was married to man who watched porn on a regular basis. He expected me to fulfill his needs at any given moment. It was never about us or me, it was about him and my duty. That entire set-up is based on an old program that is being removed by us becoming aware of its outdated and disembodied enslavement. This personal story is about becoming aware of those programs and patterns and my choice to extract them by braving what existed beyond them.

Now, I had to grow up and become a woman who knew her body. That wasn't easy because there is no real education for women and the slut-shaming prevents us from having experiences that teach us. Our needs and sexual preferences are not taught or even honored based on the old program. Being taught that someone outside of me had authority over my body, meant it wasn't safe or seen as normal to touch and to know my own body and its pleasure. That teaching began at 3 years old for me by the way my parents responded to me discovering my vagina in the bathtub with my brother.

I believe that women have been under a controlled shadow of shame. I'm exposing my own to promote a mass healing for all women and men. I'm using my muscle of self-awareness to say, "We as women deserve pleasure and for our bodies to be honored." I know this to be true and I am glad you each of you are here to learn how that eventually happened for me.

I didn't even know what I was missing but the pain of sex did make me aware that I needed to slow down and listen to my body. I don't fault the Stallion because most men do not know that it takes women longer to get their juices flowing. Many of them also do not know what we like because most women haven't had enough experience to know what to ask for. We also haven't been given permission to ask for what we want, if we do know. I am giving you all the permission if you know what you like. Say it! Men like to follow direction and they are fine with specifics, so share what you know with them.

Men, there's a sensitive nature to you where you can take feedback as ridicule. Which makes it hard to tell you what you are doing isn't working. Ridicule to men, is like rape to us. It's that serious and it does get in the way of honesty so I need both sexes to become more aware of these things for a new level of pleasure and joy to be discovered. We as women, have been in an awkward and unfulfilling sexual position in many ways. I'd like to help us get into a more pleasurable situation by sharing my process of sexual self-discovery, as a means of helping my sisters out, and my brothers too.

138

Sadly, porn is a common teacher for men and it does not honor, respect or portray the feminine and her pleasure, in my opinion. It's all about unrealistic bodies, speed, force, and defaming the feminine in many cases. I believe porn disconnects men from true intimacy and creates an addiction to a false fantasy. It harmful that porn exists because it teaches teenage boys and young men mistruths about sex. Sadly, they are the ones who become the teachers for young girls and young women. Therefore, porn becomes the authority and it tells girls their sexual needs are about pleasing the boys, and that they are supposed to like what the boys are doing to them. It took me years to learn that feminine arousal didn't look anything like a man's way of getting off. #DefundPorn

I believe sexual videos could be produced for both women and men and not be porn. I'm not a producer, actress or videographer but I could write scenes that I am sure both sexes would enjoy, as I do believe videos are a great teaching tool. But I'm not here to make sexual videos. I'm here to teach you what I have learned. Perhaps this section is its own screenplay with the help of your imagination. You can be the actress or actor in your own life by learning to get to know your body more intimately.

There are many reasons that sexual education is important. Women often experience pain and a lack of pleasure because men get excited, hard, and are ready for intercourse before our bodies are prepared for their entry. They think women have it easy and do nothing but spread her legs. That is not true. We don't have to get hard but we do need to get wet and ready for expansion. That requires men slowing down and taking their time to appreciate our bodies because that is what feels good.

It's quite painful to have a hard penis forced inside when I'm not ready for penetration. Females have learned to hide their pain and discomfort for the sake of catering to men over themselves. In many cases women are numb to their own body because of the disconnect that has resulted from; a cruel world that hasn't honored or protected the feminine. Her body brings creation to life and she herself hasn't even learned to honor her own body. I know that to be true for many women, not just me.

When I talk to men in their late 50's and early 60's who are experiencing less, or no feeling at all in their penis, they are distraught. They experience a sense of loss and begin grieving but when they talk about it and allow their feelings to be expressed, they can make it come alive again. What's interesting to ponder are the numbers of women who have gone their entire lives without pleasure and feeling much or any excitement between their legs, but have only known pain there.

Women deserve to feel the power of creation between their thighs. I'd like to share a few things I have learned to bring both sexes hope and inspiration. The average woman's body takes 25-30 minutes for all of her sexual centers to be turned on. The foreplay activates her natural lubrication and prepares her body for expansion. I'm sure you can find things online that say it takes less time, which may be the case for a percentage of women, but not for the majority. I am a woman who is telling you that our juices take time to flow and the act of foreplay can be as satisfying as the orgasm itself. Register that, and know that

I speak for many women who cannot speak up for themselves yet.

Think of the vulva as a flower. Flowers take time to open… one petal at a time. Being the complex creatures we are as women, who can carry life in our bodies, and who menstruate every 26-30 days. It's important to note that we naturally move in cycles like the seasons. It makes sense that it takes us time to open up. If we are always in a cycle, and something new wants to enter in the midst of that cycle, our bodies need time to adjust and make room for their entry. We are literally the embodiment of nature.

Men need to realize they are more like the sun to us, as an aware man. Just like the sun going behind a cloud our petals start to close when a man pulls his awareness away from us. When he diverts his attention, we feel it. That is why the conscious breathing I taught the men is important. It makes them more present and it's important for you as well. It helps both parties to get out of their minds, into their bodies, and the present moment. We as females long for their presence. It penetrates us, just like the sun. The flower can't grow or open without the sun. That is how important men are to us. Sex is an act of presence, unless we are disconnected from our bodies, and are just moving through the motions. Which is where I was at this time, with the Stallion, until I woke up to the pain that deserved to know pleasure.

I was at the start of a significant sexual learning curve. I had no idea at the time that I was in the process of reconciliation; making peace with sex by developing an intimate relationship

141

with my own body and its pleasure. Nothing I read had informed me that becoming aware and awake in the world as a woman, involved a physical embodiment of my spirit, in every area of my body. Especially, the area that brings human life into form. And this what led me to knowing and sensing my body as a sacred vessel of wisdom. Source exists in my body.

Thanks to my experiences I came to discover my Higher Self embodies through a physical, emotional, mental and spiritual integration. As for the Italian Stallion, he did gallop back into my life, again and again over the years, in the most unexpected and spontaneous ways, even though we ended up living on opposite coasts. Each time, we came back together, I was at a new place of learning. We still communicate and I admire his wickedly, clever mind but his habit of galloping at light speed between the sheets, has not given my body the presence and time to open and expand.

He hasn't gained enough awareness, in my opinion, to slow his speed. This is why learning to breathe is essential because slowing down happens in the mind first. Then the body follows. A slow, deep inhale and a slow, deep exhale are the reins that control and direct your horse power. It may take this book for the Stallion to get the message. I certainly mean no disrespect to him. In the meantime, I am grateful to him for waking me up, to an area of my life that wanted my attention. My body learning to feel pleasure took: patience, gentleness and experimentation. The next man who entered my life - brought all three.

Chapter 16
Mr. British Columbia

B.C. was my next lover, whom I considered my boyfriend after we grew close. It was serendipitous how we first met in Canada, and unexpected that we road-tripped across the United States three months later. Although our bond originally formed on a two-hour bus ride from Vancouver to the Seattle airport, our unique relationship continued by phone, until our cross-country adventure. He joined me in my major transition of moving from the east coast to the west coast.

I picked him up at the airport in Pittsburgh, PA in my SUV, with a small trailer hitched to the back and ready to head west. We had no physical touch before joining forces to drive across the country. It wasn't for the lack of desire or chemistry on both our parts. It was more about our beliefs that had us ignoring our bodies and allowing our beliefs to override our instincts. He had his sexual hang-ups, based in Christianity. I had my own shame-controlled beliefs steeped in Catholicism. One of those included a man needed to make the first move. We both ignored our natural primal instincts despite our sexual magnetism. Until months later, when I made the unconscious and unplanned decision to move within miles of his Canadian home.

B.C. turned out to be a fun and creative lover. He was also a great cook and oh so tender that I wanted nothing more than to marry him after we drove across the United States. together. It was hard when we parted ways after I arrived in California and he flew back to Canada. Still unaware of my codependency habits, my plan to live in California became altered by my unconscious beliefs when I accepted an invitation six weeks later to visit friends up north; who ironically lived close to him. I didn't preconceive I'd move there as I was busy making new friends, finding a new job and looking for a rental in California, while staying with a relative.

The unconscious belief of needing to marry again convinced me to take steps toward us being physically closer. We had such an amazing connection; I began moving through the process of what the little girl in me was brainwashed to believe; a man completed me. In order to gain sight of that belief, I had to move into the new, in order to see the old. I do wish I had been more aware as it would not have cost me my nest egg as I bought at the top of the market. I had no idea that government would kill the middle class with "Big Short" a few years later. But this is how it played out. My unconscious beliefs drove me to buy a home in a state I had never considered moving to. Until, I had better sight of my beliefs, I was blindingly guided by them.

B.C. wasn't a player but he was a lone wolf who had no intention of marrying me. As sweet as he was, he wasn't humming, "Here comes the bride" like I was in my mind. Many females are conditioned in codependency but the Millennials of today don't seem to be following in the same footsteps. Perhaps those of us from Generation X, who are the bridge between them and the Baby Boomers, have taken enough steps in a new direction that we are changing the possession of our minds, that were told things need to be one way for everybody.

There were a lot of beliefs tied into that passing of the torch from the generation before me, which included; having sex outside of marriage was shameful. I had already shifted the other belief that a man had to provide for me, by becoming financially independent before I married. But the sex outside of marriage always came with me feeling shameful as I remained disconnected from my own body and it's needs.

Women weren't respected for being financially and sexually independent. That was reserved for the masculine and not a privilege of the feminine - thanks to patriarchal rule that is now dying. Don't get me wrong, I'm all for committed relationship but I needed to first fall in love with myself and define what that would look like according to me. Before I could do that, I had to discover who I was, and that required me discovering who I was not.

Removing my identification with shame was a tough battle. In the end, I eventually won. But that was only because I continued to face my fears and go into the discomfort to free myself. Lucky for you, it may be a much shorter process as the reins of enslavement have been broken down by many who have also freed themselves. That means you can move even faster. You'll have to be patient with me because upgrading my biology from the inside out was all still new to me.

I especially liked Mr. B.C. because he had a strong yet gentle nature as a confident, alpha male; a version of masculine I had not experienced before that time. He didn't try to pounce on me. He got to know me first. All of the waiting convinced me that once we did have sex we would be together forever. Of course, none of that was discussed out loud because I was not emotionally mature to express my feelings in words. He was busy ruminating on his lone wolf status and I was busy believing we would marry. I have since learned how to share my authentic feelings and to face the fear of rejection because I no longer reject myself. At that time, I had not faced that fear to build my muscle of awareness.

Unconditional love for myself changed that habit but at this time, I was still living life out in my own head. I think it's unfortunate that so much goes unsaid in new relationships regarding needs, likes and dislikes. It's quite strange that it's more common to have sex with a stranger, (for some people) then it is to talk openly and honestly about each other's thoughts, feelings, bodies and intentions. I hope this book provokes a change.

I had learned the habit of protecting my vulnerability. Instead of facing the truth and possible rejection by sharing my feelings and body's desires. I also didn't know the alternative to my habit. Who would have known innocence had more power than denial of it? Only the new could show me the old. Until then, I was in my mind thinking that tying the knot was the only relationship deemed essential. Religious indoctrination had trained my mind to believe that my body was to be virginal, not something for me to enjoy or to love, but as an object that was for the man I would marry. But life was attempting to show me that love, respect and dignity were things I could only give to myself through a relationship with my body and heart.

There was a lot I loved about this man. We had a lot of fun together as two very playful people. He enjoyed being silly by making life a comedy; a side dish to his exquisite culinary talents. It was easy to dream of him as my husband because he had so many great attributes. His handsome face, gorgeous smile, large hands and sparkly eyes seemed to capture me like a spell. His patience and slow motion were so new to me that I was fascinated by the way he could take his time, no matter what he was doing. He had an ease about life and himself that made room for me to learn more about me and men as well.

His pace allowed me to discover pleasures of my own body and the sensitive side of men. Which I had not seen in these ways before. His approach also helped me unearth an insanely pleasurable area of my body. This happened through a very light touch and his creative nature. He was present and sensitive and tuned into my body unlike any man had ever been before. He listened with his senses, like he was tuning a string instrument, when he touched me. His presence naturally made me more aware of myself.

The discovery of this ecstatically sensual place on my body was not one of the three main areas that men usually go for. His creative playfulness brought a feather into our sex life. That light touch on this particular area of my body sent shivers up my spine. I felt a pleasure I had never experienced before and it made me purr. I came to learn that even the light touch of his fingers along that area could do the same thing to me. Not all men can bring that out in me as I later discovered. B.C. was connected to his emotional body and that impacted the sensation of his touch. It gave him a depth of presence I appreciated.

He was very aware of his own feelings which made him an exceptional lover. It was new to me to accept a man who was as sensitive as he was. I must admit a part of me needed time to expand my own thinking to respect his gentle nature, as I had learned that emotions meant weakness. And yet he was the best lover I had ever had. My mental body needed time to honestly accept that part of him.

He was extremely bright but it was his playful nature that made him more fun than men I had known before. He had a deep faith and belief and that showed in the sparkle in his eyes. He allowed creativity to flow through him and that made life fun. He even served me up on the kitchen countertop in my new home, like a main dish. He took the same time with me as he did in preparing his meals. Giving attention to the detail every step of the way. Letting the juices build and enjoying the entire process.My Canadian man had a softness that was all new to me.

He was very masculine but without the armor of toughness or a need to force and dominate. He allowed space for my own eroticism to surface. His slow approach was a welcoming change. I learned so much about my sexuality in our time together as I made a deeper bond with every inch of my skin. He treated me like a fine wine – not meant to be gulped.

Body consciousness required me getting into my body. He gave me both the space and time to do just that. Our relationship helped me to see many of my limiting beliefs and bad habits. Having been trained to become attached as a co-dependent I got to move through a process of learning detachment with him. Which was easier to do with a man who wasn't expecting me to give my power over to him. But it did break my heart when he didn't want to commit to me, in the way life told me I needed him to commit.

Learning to hold my own heart was a part of becoming emotionally and spiritually mature. And that took time to learn. It was painful for me to grow close to someone and have them leave my life. The opposite teaching of attachment was a very difficult and important lesson for me to learn over the years. My heart broke into a million pieces more than once, before I learned the one thing that could never leave me - was the unconditional love that I could extend to myself. Years of indoctrination of praying to something outside of me didn't teach me the love I sought was within me. Once, I knew my greatest love would never be lost, no matter who came and went, I could love more openly.

That is why I am now able to love each and every one of you. My own Source connection elected me to represent myself. I don't seek outer approval or believe anyone else completes me. I am sharing what I learned to inspire you to stand with me in your power too. It's your choice and independent responsibility, not mine. What I control is sharing my perspective and life experience but not how you respond to it, or how you feel and think about me.

When B.C. came into my life, he gave me the opportunity to see the old. The new is what helped me love my body more and to discover its pleasure. I saw how much I appreciated being touched with presence. It wasn't about a need to achieve an orgasm, as that was still something that would take time. But what I did discover was how much I enjoyed being touched, kissed and loved all over, without any goal or expectation in mind.

His presence and patience allowed my body the time to become more aware and awakened. I felt cherished and appreciated and that was ecstatic in itself. I heard my moans in response to how enjoyable his creative and curious touch made me feel. I got to learn how incredibly sensitive my skin is to touch, by getting out of my mind and more into my body. Moving from mind to body awareness is as different as thought is to feeling. Mr. British Columbia, who is still in my life, now two states and a border away, remains my friend. I didn't realize at the time when we were together, how much my independence and freedom meant to me. That would take me years to discover and to realize - one man and one experience at a time.

Chapter 17
The Chief

The Chief mysteriously entered my life at the local co-op about two months after B.C. exited. The Chief was a whole other version of manliness. I had never seen or dated a man who looked anything like him. Our connection began in the checkout aisle when he commented on my purchases of buffalo meat and dark chocolate. We had a nice, lively banter before I walked out of the store. I appreciated his warmth, intelligence and striking appearance.

He caught up with me outside the store to ask if he could take me to dinner. It was already dark on that cold and rainy late, fall day. I could go home and have dinner alone, which I didn't mind or I could accept the unexpected and spontaneous invite. My instincts gave me a full body, "yes!" and twenty minutes later we were sitting at a cozy table, next to a roaring fire at a beautiful restaurant along the water.

The Chief was another softer version of masculinity for me to observe and appreciate. The men I had grown up around were more aggressive alphas or completely silent. These more heart-centered men didn't seem to have something to prove or any need to dominate me. They possessed a calm and comfortable presence, yet were extremely masculine in a silent warrior-like way. Although the Canadian and the Chief were very different men, their openness, curiosity and presence provoked the same in me. What I didn't realize at the time was how these sensitive men brought a strength that was making room for me to discover both my softness and my own alpha female force.

You could say force may be more of a masculine quality. It had not been exercised in me before because I feared that power. I buried it or quickly gave it away to the man as my co-dependency taught me. Undiscovered parts of me laid hidden in the safety of fear and remained in the dark through habits. Even I had no idea more intelligence, strength and assertiveness existed in me. These dormant aspects became alive in through new relationships and experiences where I could learn to sense them and try them on for size. The embodiment of Infinite Spirit lives as a confidence that I had not known before. In order for me to find that gold, I needed to have it reflected to me and then be given a safe space to embody it.

In these romantic relationships, I had space to balance my masculine and my feminine aspects by not being forced into the roles I had known before. My former teachers instructed me to be a nice, submissive female who did what others expected of me. I grew up to an obedient woman who ended up marrying a man who forced me to give up our child and leave my favorite job, and when things ended 12 years later, he believed I didn't deserve anything we built together. That was how well-trained I was to put others before me. I gave away the gold in me to be what others told me to be. This is my walk in reclaiming what was rightfully mine all along.

The Chief was one of the wisest, tallest, fiercest looking and most gentle man, I had ever met. His piercing black Native American eyes, 6'5" frame and long, dark hair (worn pulled back) commanded my presence. His fierce, warrior power was as much about his soft heart, that projected a tangible peace, as it was about his look. He was like a giant oak I just wanted to sit underneath. I would have guessed he was ten years older than me. I was wrong. He was 20 years older, which he clarified that first night during our meal. He was transparent from the start. His Native American roots were woven in his face and felt in his sincerity and exceptional storytelling.

That first meal was more than a dinner - it was a mystical experience. I felt I had drifted off into unknown lands, where time and space dissolved. We shared a closeness that felt like we were picking up from a past life together. Our meal covered more than three courses, we touched into other dimensions within ourselves.

You know when someone has a good vibe? That's about a frequency. The Chief was of high frequency. The word vibration acknowledges spirit in the body. That is something we all need to become more aware of. My stories and transformation are about raising my frequency. The Chief upped my frequency because his depth reflected the depth within me. I felt it. That is why we surfed what seemed like an endless ocean together without leaving our seats. Time evaporated until the waiter brought us back to reality by letting us know the restaurant was closing and we needed to pay the bill.

Our relationship continued as we spent more time together. We headed into winter and found ourselves playing house for four days straight during a snowstorm. Those days included life-changing teachings for me around my body. I also learned about his and what a man without any bodily hang-ups looked like. There was a level of comfort in his nudity I had never experienced, to that extent, with any other person in my adult life. He had absolutely no shame about being in his body. He even went to the bathroom with the door open. And I don't mean taking a pee. That blew my mind in so many ways because he wasn't crass or disrespectful. Even though many people could see it that way. It was more like; this is a part of being human and there's nothing to be ashamed of.

When we were naked together, the way he studied my flower/yoni/pussy was another shocker for me. He laid next to me by turning his body the opposite direction. He wasn't in any rush. He cozied up and investigated my flower to better know it. I had never had a man who wanted to know my clitoris. He explored me with presence and patience by asking questions while touching me. I had more of a comfort with my body because of the time I spent with Mr. British Columbia and wasn't terribly embarrassed. That also had a lot to do with his own comfort. In the presence of someone who was open, honest and sincere; I could feel what that felt like. It gave me an opportunity to know my own body and the vibe of authenticity.

That afternoon, I became aware of how important it is for a man to know where a woman's clitoris is and how sensitive it is to the touch. We weren't having sex. We were in informational gathering mode. He asked questions and communicated in a way that felt nurturing and natural. His curiosity and openness allowed me to ponder my sexual organs on a deeper level. I didn't know all of the answers to his questions because I had never placed importance on getting to know that area of my body with such precision. I had learned to shame it from such an early age that I was ignorant of its power and its pleasure. I didn't know what I liked.

The Chief awakened me to the possibilities of how someone could bring my clitoris pleasure. Masturbating was the only way I brought myself to an orgasm. It was easy when I was alone but I didn't take notes. I just took care of myself. I didn't have a history of men giving me orgasms to know what I liked. In fact, no man had ever given me an orgasm. How would a woman learn about her body without the sex education needed? And truly only comes from experience. Not even a gynecologist was as open and informative as the Chief was with me. Let's face it, anyone has a better view of a woman's sacred center than she does. And that is why I found it very helpful to be engaged in an open dialog. The experience also gave me an opportunity to reunite with my clitoris and begin to heal the trauma and disconnect that had begun all the way back to me discovering its existence as a toddler.

My parents completely lost it when they saw me bent over peeling apart my own petals and peering between my thighs as an innocent toddler in the bathtub; wondering what that was on my body and why it was different from my brothers. Their violent reaction made me believe whatever was down there was bad and never to be touched again. Organized religion picked up where my parents left off when I started going to church and CCD at 5 years old. The disconnect continued through my adult life until I chose to become aware.

The Chief communicated with a gentleness that helped me to relax into my body. He then explored my pussy with his fingers for me to get a better sense of how best to instruct him. He gave me time, space, presence, and his sincere curiosity, free of force, and any expectation to perform or to serve him. It was all about my body. With that kind of attention to an area of my body that no one had ever taken the time to get to know, it permitted me to do the same. It was like a permission slip and an invitation to have a relationship with my sacred center.

Our time together made me more curious than ever to know the hidden treasure between my thighs. It's fascinating that men have the freedom to grab, adjust, stroke and to hold their penis or testicles, every day without thinking twice about it. I watched my brother as a little boy hold his penis, over his pj's, and walk down the hall every morning. The level of control I now see that has been placed over a woman's body by society programming makes me grateful for this book, and the freedom it will provoke for every woman who reads it.

If I have to put my hand on my pussy, over my clothes in public to show I have claimed its power, then so be it. I will do that on stage when you see me so that we can take a moment to applaud the pussy. It's the furthest thing from weakness and yet the word has been used to call someone weak. That needs to change now. And I'm taking a stand to make that change. Ladies, the pussy is powerful and you know it.

We will change what's come before by each one of us becoming more aware. I believe that women have the right to know their pleasure and the power that resides between their thighs. I'm a strong advocate for men and them learning to own the power in their hearts. Our work is to own our right to pleasure. That can begin on every inch of our skin and go all the way down to the tip of our clit.

I believe these realizations are steps toward balancing and respecting the feminine. My personal call-out to religious doctrine brainwashing females to believe; they do not control their own bodies and that virginal means pure. That is a lie and a means of control. The purity of our innocence is in us no matter what. Shaming our sexuality cuts us off from realizing our spiritual nature exists in our biology. I got closer to my body by being touched with the loving presence of many different men, than I ever did by a husband who assumed it was his to do as he pleased. Enslavement is not for me.

The Chief was such a great teacher. His warrior-like awareness and maturity made a lasting impression on my life. I also gained knowledge by the stories he shared. Which included what he learned from his former wife who was a tantric practitioner. She helped men with sexual issues. She had an excellent relationship with her own body and that was how he learned that each woman is unique onto herself, and that pleasing her required learning her body.

He understood that feminine sexuality was more intricate in comparison to the masculine. There was no sense of condescension or ridicule in him because he approached my body like a curious explorer. There was no wanting to dominate, possess, or to serve only himself. He didn't grow up being taught to shame his body. Therefore, he didn't see his former wife's work as anything shameful. He saw it as important and helpful to the men she served. He did find it curious how the "white man" treated the earth and their bodies with disrespect. He saw both as "one in the same" and that we are of nature. The sadness he expressed about our disconnect almost brought tears to my eyes. He carried that much care and compassion in his heart.

I never pursued tantric studies but I did choose to investigate my own body further, by finding a practitioner who could point out aspects that would help me, to better know my own clitoris. The Chief inspired me to respect and love one of the most shamed parts of my body. Only second to my heart. I found his comfort, curiosity and care refreshing, healing, initially surprising but entirely enlightening. His openness and mind/heart/body balance were contagious. Our intimacy was a gateway to more of my own personal freedom. He planted a seed in me. No, it was not sperm. It was a new perspective that began to take root and grounded me more into my own physical feminine form, that is now branching out to you… to offer you more freedom too.

Chapter 18
The Artist

Months after our intense and moving time together, the Chief vanished like a dream upon waking. He had expressed our age difference would be an issue later in life. He also prophesied I had an important mission and more learning to do before it became clear. At that time, I could only see the mission of my old habits and beliefs. The ones that were leading me towards a man to fulfill a belief system prophecy that said, I would only be complete when I was married.

The Chief brought me new possibilities and broadened my perspectives. Not just about my body but that a true warrior possessed great heart. He spoke with a developed forethought, had instant knowing, and acted with genuine compassion and consideration. He possessed a grace and an intelligence unmatched but achievable for all men. He raised the bar on many levels, in the way he touched my mind, body, and heart. I road that wave of learning into the forest where I met the next man who changed me.

I also thought I would marry him when my new best friend introduced him to me. I often refer to "The Artist" as Thoreau because he presented the great philosopher, author, and poet to me, by reading his books out loud as we laid in bed together. Thoreau was the first artist I ever dated and the only man who ever read to me. This was once again uncharted territory for me as I was raised to believe that being an artist wasn't a profession. However, our relationship took me on a creative ride of self-expression from: painting, reading, writing, to spending time in nature with more reverie. The way he lived his life was a teaching onto itself, not unlike the real Thoreau.

He was a potter, wood sculpture, painter, songwriter, guitarist, avid book reader, father, and philosopher all wrapped into on e. Like a wild man, he lived on the brink of the forest on a cliffside edge over-looking the ocean. Everything in his life was alive including his art. He would haul large pieces of wet driftwood up from the ocean, climbing over a hundred, steep, cricked steps, with an enormous, wet chunk of wood on his shoulders. He'd drop it in his front yard, where it would dry in the sun and later be carved into exquisite pieces of furniture or unique statue. He lived meekly and did things peacefully with an appreciation for life.

Since the infiltration of mega-mansions in his neighborhood, that sucked up every last piece of buildable land, his tiny trailer was the last one standing. He remained in what became an upscale neighborhood. Living simply despite the economic pressure of the landowners that surrounded him and most likely wanted him out. Their invasion did not impair his values or scare him away. What was important to him and what brought him there remained - his love and appreciation of nature.

His arms and hands were like Popeyes from his woodworking. Despite his physical strength, he was a gentle, nurturing, and well-read man, with strong opinions about many things, including the preservation of nature. I had been married to a well-read man but Thoreau took it to a new level, consuming 900-page books that he'd read more than once. His clever mind could debate me for hours with atheistic views backed by scientific facts. I got to see more of my own philosophy on life, beyond the mind. Where an intrinsic awareness, rooted in innocence, downloaded divine solutions (that I saw as common sense) to his well-articulated dilemmas and struggles of the world. I stood in my growing trust and faith in the unseen. He stood as solid in his fact-based thinking of the seen.

When our clothes came off all the debating stopped. Nature had carved him into a masterpiece. I could trace every muscle in his chest, arms, and abs with my fingers. His physical strength was balanced by his compassionate heart. This man could make passionate love to me for hours and then bake cookies, make homemade soups, and brew us a fresh pot of tea; steeping freshly picked nettles from behind his home.

His gentle, impassioned demeanor, and the way he lived his life changed me as a person. The drumming of raindrops against his tin can home, while tucked under the covers with him reading eloquent words written by Thoreau, painted new possibilities in my open mind and heart. Those moments of peaceful living would follow me home to the comfort of lounging on my lush furnishings, reflecting on the heaven awakening with me.

Thoreau made love to me with such passion and sincerity, it felt as if we were making music together. His depth of connection to the earth, combined with his strong masculine body made our lovemaking a dreamy, original work of art. His physical strength held my body with certainty. While his soft heart created spacious presence between our kisses. He'd look deeply into my eyes as if we were his painting and each move was a stroke on his canvas. Reality and imagination made manifest was the world we weaved together.

I couldn't let the enjoyment of it all last without putting my old, conditioned beliefs and habits into action. I was sure that we needed to talk about marriage, to box our magic into my learned beliefs, to make it acceptable. For who? For what? Why couldn't I relish it for what it was? We were aligned with the force of nature within us. We were dreamers together. All of it felt so right. But my mind said it was wrong.

Our dreamy relationship ended with the pressures of boxing our bliss into a package for society to consume and deem worthy. The society that lived in my mind and that created my thinking was beginning to reveal itself, as my heart broke once again. Thoreau didn't live in a box. He lived in a natural freedom; growing his greens, carving his own life into form each day as he felt inspired to do so. I had never seen such freedom and creativity. It almost seemed illegal because it was too relaxed and beautiful.

The way our bodies came together in a reverence for nature and as a freedom of creative expression was a masterpiece. The kisses were wet, slow and deep, as was his penetration when he entered me. Like the waves of an ocean, I felt the intensity as he drew inward and the contraction as he pulled out. We were like poetry in motion. Present to the intricacy of our senses through the dance of our bodies becoming one. All made possible because creativity was able to flow through us and to be expressed as us.

Sometimes it felt like we were Tarzan and Jane when we ran through the forest together. There was a sweet innocence and a wellspring of passion in our adventures together. It wasn't a love that required a marriage certificate. It was simply love for life and one another. I had the privilege to fall into the depths of a creative genius who could lose himself in: massive books, beautiful paintings, elaborate wood carvings, or in the strings of his guitar while he sang to me. He never seemed rushed, late or impatient about anything. He remained present and grateful, living simply and happily. Lack didn't exist in his reality. He lived month to month and was generous with everything he had.

I had no idea I was sharing time with a mostly reclusive person. That I was having the opportunity to peer into his private world to see life outside the box. Was it through our experience together as to how I came to live in the mountains, in my own isolation many years later? It was certainly one of many pivotal experiences that helped me to understand and accept the part of me who cherishes both: time alone and living in nature. Thoreau may have planted many seeds in me by displaying life outside of the: rushing, stressing, accumulating and keeping up with the Joneses narrative. Which impressed upon me his unshakeable authenticity.

Here I am years later, living happiness not determined by others but rather by choice. A life that was set in motion by deciding I would live as my highest and greatest potential. Not knowing what honing to greater perfection would look like. But now I see that my values of truth, clarity, connection and human understanding; help other others to become more clear about themselves - through the clarity of my communication about

163

myself. As an author, podcaster, lion tamer and inspirational teacher; I empower others to put words to their feelings and personal experiences they could not otherwise express themselves. I crystalize thoughts and affirm ideas by bringing awareness to things that may be on everyone's mind, but are left unspoken. My creativity, life experience and wellbeing has determined my personal fulfillment. I now live in a freedom that I believe is everybody's birthright.

Thoreau remains a dear friend of mine to this day. I love his mind and heart and feel blessed to have him in my life. Our profound and intimate three-month relationship brought me expanded levels of awareness, magic, wonder, and creativity. He was truly an inspiration to the writer and hermit in me. Our time together was a living fairy tale that included moments that remain with me to this day.

One of those moments, was in the snow-covered forest behind his tin can home. Where bald eagles would nest and often speak to me, as clearly as the forest herself, in ways my heart understood. That day, the sun was shining on my joyous face as my head was tilted upward. I was catching giant snowflakes on the tip of my tongue. My arms were outstretched and I was slowly spinning in a circle. Just like the snowflakes themselves that spiraled into my open mouth. Those playful moments where I honored the child within, I felt my innocence wildly alive in me.

Today, I make no apology for playing, dreaming and keeping the wonder fully alive in my life. Thoreau captured my state of transcendence in that magical forest, by painting a picture of me floating above the ground, drifting upward into the trees, in a sheer white dress. His art is a treasured memory that hangs on a wall in my home. It always brings a smile to my face, in memory of the magic that exists within me. And as a reminder of how the beauty of nature brings it out in me. My heart is full of gratitude for the Artist and the wealth of teachings he bestowed upon me, in the way he lived his life. "Wealth is the ability to fully experience life." -Thoreau.

Chapter 19
Realizations Along the Way

These men by their loving temperament helped me to begin to heal lifelong unconscious habits of self-rejection and self-shaming my body and heart. When I was in-tune with my body, I experienced the flow of creativity as a life force that's expressed through me, in its own unique way. Just like these words that capture my life moments have become a book that now flow into your life. My body and hearts pleasure fuel my creativity. These natural aspects of my human nature had been controlled and shamed by people outside of me. As a result, I learned to deny them. I had not opened to the artist in me, until I spent intimate time with the Artist himself.

I sincerely value the quality time I spent with each of these very special men. They were extremely smart, compassionate, gentle, strong, and masculine. Their presence enriched my life greatly. Each one of them said and did unique things to me, with me and for me. Some of those thoughtful acts were: running me baths, cooking me meals, and making love to me in new and unexplored ways with patience and presence. They encouraged me to learn more about myself because they didn't make it all about them. They were all alphas who possessed both physical and inner strength. They had developed emotional, physical, and spiritual bodies. Their mental body intelligence is what first attracted me and intrigued me to a higher intelligence. These men could feel and express their intelligence with heart. Their strength of softness made space for me to discover more of who I am.

When I look back on it all, I realize how my spiritual nature was being more embodied in their presence by the way they treated me. I was waking up to my body consciousness and learning to sense my heart more clearly because they lived that way themselves. They educated me with compassion not condescension. They honored me in ways that helped me to honor myself.

Through religion and societal conditioning, I crucified my sexuality and lost connection with my body at a very young age. Since our physical and emotional bodies communicate our spiritual nature, I was cut off from knowing myself on a deeper level. Until, I brought my spirit into my biology through these intimate encounters. They opened my mind and strengthened my connection with my Higher Self. Their compassionate nature helped me to heal and retrieve aspects of me that had been denied and shamed away. Their ability to nurture me and to sense with their heart created a safe space for me to return to me.

That didn't mean I didn't face conflicting and shameful thoughts in my mind that arose before, during, or after sex. With the loving space that these three, heart-centered, warriors provided me, I could better identify my old beliefs and make new choices. I made mistakes along the way, but they weren't as great as the enslavement of beliefs that caused me great pain and suffering. I gained more sight of the old control system and my patterns in each new experience. By seeing the old and feeling the discomfort of those thoughts in my body, I had an opportunity to create change. I had choice over habit.

My process was one of expression, experimentation, integration and transcendence. It was my infinite spirit or inner spark making its way into my body. Each new experience brought realizations. All I needed was the courage to handle my emotions by letting them inform me. Some of the emotions that came up needed to be discharged. I had an opportunity to feel through them, by holding my own heart and letting go of the old emotions that surfaced to be cleared.

I continued to remain open and to weed out disempowering beliefs and thoughts along the way. When I was willing to call myself out, new solutions were birthed from within me. My heart and body were being given the respect they deserved. The respect the men gave to me helped me to give it to myself. By learning to hold my own heart, instead of quickly giving it away to a man, I was given choice over habit. These men weren't expecting me to give away my power so I had no choice but to learn how to carry and hold it myself.

I didn't know where any of my new choices would lead. I had to get comfortable with making mistakes. Being the explorer constantly put me in new, uncharted territory. In the unknown I was alchemized. The more my heart and body healed, the more clear I became. The more my mind and heart opened, the more new experiences came my way.

Life was blowing my mind by challenging my beliefs about: love, life, and relationship. I was discovering who I was underneath all of the patters and programs, by discovering who I was not. Men who were vulnerable, nurturing and compassionate were showing me a balance of masculine and feminine. It was in the way they embraced their heart and mind. Moving west propelled my personal growth to new levels, as new possibilities outside of - rigid and traditional, "suffering-required," workaholic ways existed. These men, who are some of my hero's, opened me up to a new relationship with my mind, heart and body.

Chapter 20
My Girlfriends Husband

Yes, that is what I said. It blew my mind too. My next learning experience came as an invite from another new close friend. It was an unusual one. That's for sure. I had opened my mind a lot to consider a sexual relationship with a married man. An invitation that came from his wife herself. My girlfriend of about a year at that time, was about 20 years older than me. She approached me about sleeping with her husband, who was about 15 years younger than her. She was going through hormonal changes and was no longer interested in having sex with him. Although my friendship had only been with her, I considered her proposal in support of my sexual learning curve.

I was open, curious, and willing to challenge my beliefs around love and life, and my body and mind. And this is what landed on my doorstep next. Her proposition initially blew my mind. Even I was shocked. After some deep contemplation, I accepted her offer.

I didn't know that an ulterior motive was attached to her request that had to do with using me, to create a rift in their relationship so that she could divorce him. I'm not sure if I believe her when she says that wasn't her initial motive, as she later explained it was more about her husband getting the sexual attention he was seeking. That was the storyline I had initially bought into without realizing she was more calculated in her moves. She saw my naivety and the deep seeking I was doing in my life as I shared my growth process with her. I would have never thought I was being played by someone I trusted. But life has taught me some very tough lessons about others peoples motives not being pure like my own. This was one of those experiences.

The only reason I even mention this disastrous scenario is because I understand that opening up, to new ways and new things, requires trial and error. Which means taking risks and making mistakes to learn what works and what does not. Some of my toughest lessons have come from people closest to me. People not worthy of my trust but because they were family or close friends, I didn't see their negative motivations. Life will always be a learning process. Today my mistakes are course corrected more quickly. But I did have to learn that mistakes were a part of gaining knowledge. It would have been easier to leave this particular relationship out of my book because I don't like to remember it. But I wanted you to see where my curiosity and adventure took me, and how I could have never predicted many of the twists and turns.

I trusted this friend and thought I was helping her out, while exploring new possibilities around my sexuality; outside of the box that my unconscious patterns wanted to so desperately drag me back into. The pounding message in my mind was about being married again. I understand that the male readers may not know what that pressure feels like, other than being on the receiving end of it. Programming begins at such an early age we don't even realize it's being wired into us. Playing mommy with baby dolls and cooking meals with our own home kitchen sets at 4, 5 and 6 years old is where it begins. Then it morphs into the teaching that "sex and marriage" go hand and hand.

I was working hard to unwire, uproot, and change what others put into my mind, to discover who I was and what did work for me underneath it all. It was easier to return to my familiar, habitual beliefs. That is why I accepted her unconventional offer. It immediately forced me to remove the marriage piece and it gave me the opportunity to have safe sex with someone to continue my exploration of my own body.

My girlfriend was a very smart and spiritual woman. She was the daughter of a surgeon, well educated in elite prep schools, a home owner and business owner. She was interesting, open and financially secure. I was in the process of opening up more each day as new realizations will do that to you. I was more curious about my sexuality as my biology was moving me into deeper realization. This new relationship was like playing a trick on my mind by removing the marriage condition. It was a unique and unexpected opportunity outside of my conditioning.

That was the place I was coming from so I didn't sense the issues or foresee the calculated moves that would later play out by ulterior motives. Things eventually intensified for all three of us. Her intent was not pure which drove calculated moves that lacked transparency. I was too busy being caught up in my own process of internal change that I didn't see things going sideways but I did later face the storm of it all. Her husband was a loner and not a spiritual seeker, like me or her. She portrayed him as a soft and kind man. Although he appreciated nature and cooked their meals, he was hardened on the inside. Being highly empathetic I could feel his inner anger as if he was pissed at the world. I let my rational mind override my gut instincts that were posing a reluctancy to move forward. That was due to my bad habit of moving toward things that didn't feel right or good.

When I did step into a sexual relationship with him, I discovered the source of his anger stemmed from being adopted and having never processed his feelings of abandonment, that lingered in his body like a stench. Even when he was laid back and easy going there was still an intensity from his unexpressed emotions wafting in his auric field. It was like an unconscious chip on his shoulder.

Our sexual encounters aren't anything to write home about, other than me noticing how much more comfortable I was with my own body and wanting to explore bringing pleasure to a man more for my own enjoyment than his. Sure, he loved it but I was more conscious of how much I enjoyed the touch and feel of things I was once just in the motion of performing. I also got to see the power of my sensual nature without being intimidated or automatically shaming myself. By staying aware, versus going into shame. I observed the impact my touch and sensuality had on him. Not only from his physical response but from the things he said to me. He couldn't stop talking about the level of arousal he experienced when we were together. With no goal of marriage, I let his body be a toy box for me to play with. I had fun.

He wasn't bringing me to the same heights of ecstasy but our relationship was serving a purpose for me that was entirely different. This time, I could vividly see my mind thinking about the need for commitment the moment my clothes came off. It was like a switch that went on. Now I could see it clearly. I was also at an age that made me contemplate having a child and that was something I could talk to him about because it wasn't about boxing our relationship but rather hearing my feelings and thoughts out loud without expectation on him for fulfilling my desires. It felt safe to dream about being a mother without having him run away like men can do when you mention commitment and family.

This relationship was more of an education about my body, my boundaries and my sexuality. I came to see how much I enjoyed a man's body. With no expectations attached I played for my own self enjoyment and he obviously enjoyed my play. As for boundaries, I may spend the rest of my life refining them as they aren't a one-size fits all king of thing. Learning to hold them and to adjust them in each situation requires awareness and maturity. I did notice that becoming more open was a process of having no boundaries. The harder part was in doing the opposite which was establishing firm boundaries in the situations that required them. I had to drop people-pleasing habits to hold strong boundaries and that took self-love. Until then, it wasn't easy. People-pleasing led me to over-extending myself, which I did in this relationship.

We aren't taught boundary laying as we grow up. Because of my learned behavior in codependency, I would default to people-pleasing in relationships. In this one, I did it when my girlfriend suggested her husband rehabilitate at my home after his surgery. He was a cyclist who had an injury years prior to us meeting that now required a serious surgery. I found myself in the role as caretaker over a 4-to-5-week period of time. That was not my responsibility and I would not have agreed to care for him - had I been the woman I am today.

The programming of "Be a nice girl and put others first" was a program I was dragging around. What went along with that belief were thoughts that I was a bad person if I didn't sacrifice myself for someone else's needs. That conditioning was put in place when I was an innocent child. I learned to protect my parents in order to keep myself safe. Making people-pleasing a deep unconscious pattern that was tied to my own survival. That belief also supported the idea that someone outside of me was the boss of my life and my body.

The other piece playing out was physical pain in my stomach that I felt from religious guilt when I had sex outside of marriage, or outside a committed relationship that I believed was leading to marriage. I would quietly crucify myself as my own living penance. None of these thoughts felt good inside my body. They actually caused me physical pain because they were daggers of judgments. Why couldn't I just enjoy sex and learn my body with a man without having to hate myself? The answer to that question could be directed toward organized religion and societal programming and their dominion over the masses.

Thanks to our design as humans, we can evolve out of false narratives by daring to imagine and to move into the unknown through new experiences to sense something new. Thanks to meditation and intentional living, I learned to slow my mind and to reprogram my thinking by catching sight of thoughts that were directing me. The more I learned how to stay in the present moment, the more I was able to identify where the pain was coming from within my own body. Bringing presence into my biology was its own healing salve.

I liked the loyalty and constancy of a committed relationship but it was always about marriage as the destination, not just companionship. It was about ownership and codependency, along with the religious dogma tied to someone outside of me determining the law over my body. All of those ideals weren't who I was, they were programs placed on me as systems of conformity and control. Apparently, I needed to walk into the discomfort of shame over and over again, to eventually find freedom. I was engaging in the things that frightened me, until they no longer had control over me. Life would assist me in doing that with new experiences that allowed me to express, experience, integrate and then transcend my former beliefs. That took time and taking risks where I felt the contraction of an inner crucifixion. But by staying in the present moment, I could see that nobody was crucifying me, other than me. Liberation was mine through that alchemical process.

In the end, my girlfriend's jealousy and calculated moves, combined with his unhealed trauma of abandonment, played into my habit of over-extending myself and like a bomb it all exploded. When he woke in the middle of the night at my house and realized I wasn't lying next to him, he got triggered. I had moved out to the sofa to try to get some sleep because I couldn't sleep next to him. He woke in the middle of the night and felt abandoned. He pulled out a gun in the midst of rage. When I heard his deep voice, I opened my eyes to find him standing over me with a gun in his hand. I had never seen a gun in real life before but I had seen a man in rage more than once. You can imagine how frightened I was.

The whole dramatic incident sent them both out of my life at that moment. She came and picked him up after he called her, once he was done screaming at me. I kept asking him what was wrong as tears of terror ran down my face. I didn't see or speak to either one of them again, until many months later when she reached out to me after she divorced him. That's when she apologized and confessed to me that she had used me to extract him from her life. She also admitted that she got jealous and didn't appreciate that I wasn't spending as much time with her anymore. She also made snide comments about how sexually aroused he felt with me, and how it even surprised him. In other words, he was being transparent with her. Neither he or I realized she was being vindictive with us.

It hurt me to learn that she betrayed me from the start. And that she was jealous of me and had no concern about my welfare in it all. She had used me to free herself from him. I felt both sad and angry and didn't even mention how terrified I was when he drew a gun on me. I had been used to going through pain and suffering on my own that I didn't concern her with my pain. It was also a habit of mine to blame myself for other people's misery and since she took the route of making it out to be the villain a part of me played along. I don't excuse myself for my part of not holding better boundaries. My openness isn't something I will apologize for as it was the doorway for me to learn and grow.

Quite honestly, I believe it was her jealous that stirred the pot and combusted the whole thing, as she had the power to craft the idea and to blow it up. And she did. Sure, he had major issues that needed addressing but she kept him financially comfortable and distant enough that his issues didn't become hers. I was the one that brought emotional vulnerability to the relationship and I saw how tender he was inside. That's probably the piece she was most jealous about because sex wasn't her thing. His heart growing close to me was most likely the issue. She wasn't transparent with her vulnerability or with her plan.

That is why every adult should be working on themselves because unprocessed emotions become a pain that is manipulative, explosive or physically debilitating to our bodies. The need to heal is to be respected as a natural process that we can no longer deny. Emotional healing takes time but it also transcends us into higher states of awareness.

As for my girlfriend, I expressed my feelings to her openly. I then needed time to think about our friendship. Eventually, I forgave her and we moved on as friends her weren't as close. Her husband moved out of town so I never saw him again. The whole experience was another set of lessons and new knowledge that I gained and took with me. I needed to work on my boundaries and to know my limits, and to apply a more stringent self-care regimen to support my body and mind. I also learned that a three-way relationship required far more communication than a two-way relationship. There was too much drama in it for me to be interested in ever going there again.

Witnessing the issues that each of us needed to address, made me aware of the work that only I could do on myself. A friend once said to me, when you move out of your parents' house, it's not about no longer needing parents, it's about learning to parent yourself. That's exactly what I needed to do. My sexual relationship with my girlfriend's husband, triggered my sense of security when he pulled out a gun. I felt attacked, betrayed and abandonment when they both turned on me and exited my life, without even a care. The experience gave me an opportunity to heal more of my own wounds and to be more loving to myself. That would require me to change the habit of betraying and abandoning myself first. I wasn't to blame for everyone else's unhappiness.

Life had originally taught me to care more about others, than myself. I was now learning the opposite; to care for myself and to hold my own heart first. When others left, that meant I needed me more than ever. I had to learn to become my best friend and to love the vulnerable parts of me even when others could not. Learning to unconditionally love for myself took a lot of work. I had a long way to go.

The friendship with my girlfriend is still evolving. I welcomed her back into my life on a deeper level years later, when she made a sincere plea of wanting to be closer to me. She had become more aware of how she dismisses her own emotions and the emotions of others with her popular phrase, "It's just water under the bridge." I honor my feelings as a guidance system once I healed more of my past. But she being highly intellectual, and in the habit of allowing her feelings to flow away without having dealt with them first, didn't mean they went away. A closer friendship was a bit of a challenge because she didn't know how to hold her own feelings and pushed away when a deeper connection was possible. She doesn't trust me with her feelings because she doesn't trust herself. You can only grow so close to someone who doesn't let you in more. She may think her feelings go away because she excuses them with her intellect but they don't. The body eventually processes them out. Which can happen when we least expect it as opportunities for healing constantly present themselves through our relationships and interactions.

We grow wiser and kinder together when we can honestly look at ourselves; both individually and together. In this situation, me and my girlfriend each took responsibility for our parts. I allowed forgiveness and the willingness to grow, to lead us back together. Unfortunately, she can't be entirely honest about her feelings. Most recently, the loving things she had said to me to set our relationship on a new path, were discarded by her as if they were meaningless. I found it disheartening and although her habits have nothing to do with me, it still hurt. She doesn't hold her own heart to be able to hold her heartfelt words in a place of integrity.

Smart as a whip and as sly as fox, is what you can get from a sharp intellect. Being vulnerable is tough and it shows strength. It takes work to break out of old conditioning because it requires us to engage with the things that frightens us. I get it. I can love her where she is and establish boundaries that cherish my own heart. With that said, I understand that sleeping with her husband didn't have many sexual highlights, however there were a lot of teaching moments for me. As for the sex, I did have my own breakthrough in desiring a man's body in ways I had not experienced before. You could say that the removal of expectations that came with the conditioning around relationships made more room for me to play. The penis had a whole new intrigue when nothing was expected of me, other than enjoying it. Perhaps that was its own icing on the cake of this sexual encounter.

Chapter 21
Jesus

I took a spontaneous trip to Peru, which was prompted by a screening of a movie featuring rituals called the Munay-ki. After watching the documentary, I went home that night with a certainty that I needed to receive the "rites of passage" by the Incan elders themselves in Peru. Why I wanted to do such a thing was beyond me. Try not to judge me for following my peculiar instincts. My decisions didn't even make sense to me at that time but something felt right about following them. I found a group online headed to Peru to receive the 9 rites of passage/initiation called the Munay-ki, at various sacred sites throughout the Andes led by the elders who were known as shamans. I had never thought about going to Peru until that moment and for that specific reason.

A month later, I was sitting in a circle of what felt like kindred spirits with the medicine men who would initiate me. Our group was led by an arrogant man who many were fawning over. My curiosity was directed toward the shamans and the rites of passage, and not him. They had a magnetism and wore vibrant, woven fabrics that made them stand out. On the night of our arrival, we learned that our hotel was overbooked, and a small group of us were transferred to a different location. I enjoyed the smaller, more intimate group that I became a part of. Without the leader and his need for admiration, my new location opened a deeper connection to the Andes, and to my experience as a whole.

The following day, I met one of the late arrivals. His name was Jesus. I befriended him and brought him up to speed on the layout of the lodge and the day's activities. He and I became instant friends and would sit together at times. I made a few other close friends as well. The group was from all over the world. There were many interesting people between the ages of 28-65, from various backgrounds that included doctors, attorneys, world travelers, and soul seekers.

As the days progressed, I felt myself sinking deeper inward as the elaborate initiations and ceremonies shifted and altered my consciousness. My state of being was being transformed and the present moment was becoming more and more my new normal. I knew what that felt like from a paranormal experience I had in the River Jordan years earlier. I lived in a state of presence for an entire day after my experience that it made a lasting impression on me. It was ecstatic to feel the breeze and to hear every sound as if I was spying on life. Peru seemed to have the same effect on me. The landscape of the majestic Andean mountains; the longest continental mountain range in the world, was the backdrop to my mystical experience of hiking to sacred sites and participating in elaborate rituals and ceremonies, packed with prayer and intention.

We carried our own mesa's that the shamans instructed how to make, by bundling 13 rocks; each representing a wound or a gift to heal and transform, wrapped in a colorful tapestry. In helping to heal those wounds the shamans would bang their bundles (mesas) against our bodies individually, during each initiation, while chanting prayers in their native tongue. It was quite an experience to be banged with a bundle of rocks, up and down the front and back of my body. They also spit a spicy fluid around us as a part of the ritual, which also included burning an elaborately crafted paper bundle, at the end of each ceremony to release the prayers, our burdens and old baggage. The initiations didn't free me from doing my personal work but they did: elevate my consciousness, send prayers for my healing, and prayers to my ancestors, who had passed down their unresolved burdens and beliefs for the next generation to heal. We were all participating in our individual and family lineage healing.

When our group made our way to Machu Picchu a week later, I spontaneously decided to stay the night. I left the group because I wanted to climb the sister mountain next to Machu Picchu the following morning. The only way to climb Huayna Picchu was to be one of the first 400 visitors they would let through each morning. I was nervous about leaving the group and was afraid I might not find my way back by train the next day. But something in me led the way with a certainty. I faced my fears by feeling them in my body, while hearing my rational mind insist it made more sense to stay with the group. I allowed my instincts to lead me. Deep breathing helped me through the contraction I felt in my body, from the anxiety my thoughts inflicted upon me. I went ahead and let the organizer know that I would be back the following afternoon before our next ceremony, and then I went off on my own.

I headed into the quaint town as my group boarded the bus. When I rounded the corner of the main street I ran right into Jesus. I was happily surprised to see a familiar face. His face lit up when he saw me. He continued down the cobblestone street toward me. He had the same plan in mind, to hike the sister mountain the following morning. We smiled at each other in delight knowing we were in good company and decided to share a meal and a hotel room together.

That night under a full moon, Jesus pulled me close as we both stared up into the glowing, radiant sphere, orbiting outside our hotel room window. We had formed a bond on that initial day when he arrived and our friendship had grown over the first week of initiations. I felt comfortable being held in his arms, as we both admired the enormous moon perched between the two famous mountains.

His unexpected kiss to my neck and the sweet words he whispered into my ear, led to our divine lovemaking that night. It was one of the most soulful encounters, imbued with grace, that we both felt when he entered me. I would have never imagined a man, who was a stranger just a week prior, and from the opposite side of the globe, would feel so lovingly close to me. I wasn't in the practice of one-night stands and this wasn't anything like that. The way Jesus looked deeply into my eyes and saw me; was as if the moon opened a passageway that magnified our connection. I can't explain it but our language barrier dissolved that evening and a deeper bond formed between us that still exists today. He was passionate and tender in the way he kissed my entire body and, in the way he held me. He wrapped not only his arms around me but his heart held me close. It felt as if we were suspended in light the way our bodies were lit up from the inside out.

We had spent seven days prior to that evening, receiving codes that transform the human energy field through energetic transmissions; an initiatory practice called the Munay-ki. I wasn't studied in those rites but the transmissions took on a new form in our lovemaking that night. Consider it an embodiment that was like being zapped by love in every cell of my body. I truly think that the sacredness of lovemaking and its ability to connect us to our spirit, has been over-shadowed, lost, forgotten and twisted into something shameful, forced or obligatory. I found consensual sex with present partners to be a natural alchemy of healing and transformation. The wisdom of this truth was not something I had ever imagined or believed but rather something I experienced.

Jesus nicknamed me the Goddess of Love that night and confessed a magic he felt when our bodies came together. Although the nine rites of passage were about attuning our body and realigning our DNA with its fuller helix structure, our unexpected lovemaking became its own rite of passage, for me. I peeled back another layer of sexual shame, in the communion of a loving and present man, who honored the sacred in himself and within me. I was beginning to remember that sexuality wasn't a perverted act outside of marriage - it was a conscious communion of love in physical form. It was about honor, appreciation, balance and presence. The key was consciousness.

Some organized religion corrupted that wisdom and perhaps buried the truth in the Vatican vaults but they did not remove remembrance of my divine connection to Source. Both my idealistic and inherited beliefs were challenged by the truth of what my heart and body felt that night, as my mind processed the conflict and contraction of my learned beliefs, that desperately wanted to enforce guilt as punishment. I observed those thoughts with my muscle of awareness and I transcended the past, by allowing my sensual feminine that flowed through our act of sex to speak louder than the lies that had clouded the sacredness of what we had just shared. My new experience shed light on the old and allowed the alchemy of new realizations to take form.

It wasn't in one fell swoop that I was freed from sexual shame but something significantly loosened its grip on me that night. My intentional living and the physical embodiment of more of my spirit was supported by new experiences. The framework of my daily practices each morning, is what kept me in alignment and drew to me the new experiences and opportunities, which spiraled new realization into my biology. Divinity was no longer a prayer to be sent skyward; it was a living embodiment to be integrated with each new experience and realized in physical form. I now see devotion as an honoring and an embodying of my Higher Self in physical form as I choose to live for the highest good of all.

My former religion would have never permitted me to believe that I was divine, holy, sacred or wise. I was controlled as a sinner and told that sacred was reserved for one man, who was portrayed bleeding on a cross. I was taught how to crucify myself with judgments as hell was my destiny and living embodiment. I learned unjust teachings as an innocent child that became cemented as an enslavement of guilt, shame and pain. It was difficult for me to sleep at night as a child because I would lie awake thinking that when I closed my eyes I might go to hell. The teachings of unworthiness would take me a concentrated period of time to unlearn, and require all of my focus to uproot them. I had ingested false narratives and to replace those teachings, I had to embody the true nature of who I am.

Today, I believe the faith I was raised in is criminal. You can have different opinions as religion has brought many hope and faith. Please don't fight me on what I know is true for me. I'm not saying religion is bad or good. I'm merely living out my experience for my own personal liberation. I personally know how much freedom, peace, pleasure and joy religious doctrine robbed from my life through the manipulation of my consciousness. I also know how much effort and work it takes to remove the lies as I am driven by the fullest liberation of my mind, body, and heart. Since this lover's name is Jesus, it's apropos' to convey my realizations around religion and sex as my own living scripture. The real message that I believe Christ stood for was to example a potential as a living embodiment of unconditional love; a realization possible for every single human on earth. Not just for men or just for him, but a potential for all of mankind. Not as a religion with a middleman but as a way of life as a living practice.

It's a heroic feat to love oneself unconditionally but when you do, you can't help but to love everyone else. You might say that's the God in you and that you came to love yourself as that Infinite Spark… unconditionally. A job that can't be done without heart. But it is clearly a choice, not forced upon you. You chose "it" because "it" gave you the free-will to choose.

When I chose, "it" in the form of my Higher Self or Infinite Spirit, I gave up my teeny, tiny world all boxed up by others to live in a much larger world - within me. My Higher Self brought me into experiences that didn't make sense to my mind but on the other side of each of them, I was more loving and accepting of myself and more open to perspectives and possibilities that I never considered or knew existed. Just like receiving the Munay-ki initiation or leaving a large group while traveling aboard to have my own adventure. My experiences led to more unexpected situations that changed my perception.

I thank Paramahansa Yogananda who first inspired me through his book, "The Autobiography of a Yogi." It turned out that my modern-day version of self-realization required me to heal the relationship with my own body and heart. Yogananda came out of the womb remembering who he was. I, on the other hand, was forced into forgetfulness upon my entry. A lineage of programming inherited at birth and reinforced through my upbringing; would be the box I would later bust out of. I would have never considered realizations would come through falling in love with my body and making peace with sex and my feminine nature. A willingness to trust the process was another important understanding for me to learn because my mind was used to the predictable world of certainty.

My sexual experiences with kind, strong, gentle, compassionate and conscious men, helped me to embody more of my Spirit. My sensual nature awakened and grew as its own unique, divine aspect of who I am. In the acceptance and appreciation of my feminine form, my voice deepened and my playfulness bubbled up from a deep well within me. My life used to be all about me and my worries, and now all my heart wants to do is to selfishly reach out and care about you. My trip to the Andes was more about making love to myself through another,

189

who could loving hold my heart and body as tenderly as he held his own. Together we merged in that deep loving place and healing happened.

Chapter 22
The Captain

A couple of months after returning from Peru, I landed in the middle of the Pacific Ocean on the Big Island. The moment I stepped off the plane I felt an amplified energetic vibe. It was tangible in my body. The light headedness I experienced was like a waking dream. I could feel my multidimensional self. Peru, had its own "between the worlds" feel to it but much more earthy and grounded. Kona lifted me up and into an expanse that made me feel like I was on a carpet ride through the ethers. I was more open to my emotional body because I was learning to trust my body and feelings again. That put me in direct contact with my spiritual nature and it's why I was immediately aware of my dreaminess the moment I stepped off the plane.

The book writing class that brought me to Kona became secondary to what the island had in store for me. I had signed up for the workshop because I got the sense that I would be writing a book one day. My rational mind wanted to take the practical steps to accomplish that mission. Seemed logical to me at the time. But as it turned out my trip had nothing to do with the writing workshop. I wouldn't need a class to learn to write a book, I was a natural at expressing my thoughts on paper. My job was to heal and to sample life and then share my experiences that would help others become more clear about themselves. I wouldn't be known for grammatical perfectionism, but rather for my experiences and realizations recorded as a living journal. My life would empower others to put words to their own experiences and to discover their own voice. That would happen later (which is now) but this was then.

A tall, dark and handsome native Californian, who resided in Kona, greeted me with his glistening Big Island smile and sun-kissed skin. His muscular arms were holding a sign with my name on it. Lucky me! It turned out that he was driving the van that would take me to my hotel. When I waved at him, he boisterously projected his thoughts into the breezy island air, "Aren't you a sight for sore eyes! Am I in the presence of an angel, or what!"

The twinkle in his eyes as he spoke those big-hearted words to me, put a smile on my face and hinted an adventure was in store for me. I learned on our drive to the hotel that he was the captain of his own boat. Once a week or twice a week he did pick-ups at the airport and that is how he landed in my life. My mind was convinced I'd be nestled away in my workshop, until the Captain seized my certainty with an unexpected invitation. He asked, if I would like join him the next morning for a day at sea. As a responsible adult, I felt committed to the class I had signed up for and was certain I would not waiver from my plan.

Yet a part of me knew, "the universe was always conspiring in my favor" in alignment with my highest and greatest potential. Sure, my logical mind always thought it knew best but the quantum field of possibilities was expanding my awareness with new opportunities. There were far more important things for me to learn outside of my class but my pragmatic mind would not have the proof in advance. My right and left brain were now at war. "I am responsible. I paid for the workshop. I am committed

192

to going. I don't waste money or take things for granted." The right hemisphere of my brain got dreamy and felt excited about "a day at sea." I didn't know what that meant, other than being in a boat, but I did feel all giddy inside about the adventure and the mystery of it all.

I thanked him for the invite when I got to my hotel and told him I'd think about it. I headed to my class that evening with his invitation tugging at my heart, like a dog excited to go on a walk. The coaxing of a part of me, was dancing in excitement, like "get the leash, come on, get the leash, let's go!" That was my emotional body prodding me and I could feel it in my stomach and heart. I kept returning to my mental body, remaining calm and focused on my class. You could see the pride of my pragmatism, with the stroke of my hand smugly smoothing over the top of my hair, as if to keep everything in its proper place. That's right, 'everything is under control.' The weekend agenda was passed around and I became silent inside. I noticed my emotional body wasn't excited about the material being covered the following day. It didn't seem like anything major or important was being taught. I had the feeling of 'blah.'

When I got back to my room, I called the Captain and confirmed that I would be joining him the next morning. The two sides of my brain had it out with each other during that call. The left side felt duped as I hung up the phone. It was as surprised as I was. The creative, right side, explorer won. I had mixed feelings about giving into my excitement and not taking responsibility for something I deemed was important. Those kind of heart over mind battles were painful if I let myself overthink it. My instincts made a decision. My mind would need to back off with the help of deep breathing. That, and focusing on the things I was grateful for would help my heart feel light.

Wallah! Cue the scene and imagine beauty beyond belief. Because that is what I saw the next morning as I was whisked away on a beautiful boat into the pristine waters of the Hawaiian Islands, as the sun greeted the day. The Captain was a strong, happy man with a smile that said, "You can live wherever and however you wish. Look how happy I am living my bliss." The joy in his face and the beauty all around him was heaven on earth. We went so far out into the ocean I could no longer see land. And yet I felt safe with him because of his sincere and open heart. Plus, he had greeted everyone at my hotel, and it was clear that he was well-liked and well-known. He had a relaxed vibe about him. I felt no pressure, just an intrigue about the alluring sense of mystery and magic in his eyes.

It was the two of us surrounded by the vast ocean, dreamy blue sky and a vibrant sun that made everything sparkle. When he stopped the boat, he dropped his fishing line into the water. After clicking it into place he flashed me a huge smile. I remember that moment like it was yesterday because there was a deafening silence as the calm sea rocked our boat like a bassinet. The beauty and quietude penetrated me with a depth of peace that felt euphoric. It's amazing how nature can throw me down and take me into the depths of the present moment. Grace is power. Every little detail becomes amplified in the present moment.

My love affair with nature awakened more deeply with Thoreau but it was years prior on a trip to Sedona (you'll have to read about in my first book) that woke me up to the nature within me. It is the most important relationship to me. Nature transforms me and clears my mind of all thoughts, worry's, and wants. It beckons me into a deep surrender of the present moment. It brings me to the voice in my heart and I hear it more clearly. What's not to love about that?

There is nothing like the present moment and yet we hardly spend time there. Until we develop healthy habits and practices that reunite us with the only place that truly exists. It's a spiritual experience to be in the present moment. As your spiritual body develops, you'll be spending more time there too. It's the only place our spiritual nature resides – in the here and now. Our emotional and physical body is what takes us there. With that said, the Captain was perceptive and saw the power nature had over me. He smiled and observed me glowing in gratitude. I felt as big as the sky and as fluid as the ocean. I melted into the beauty all around me through my wide-open heart.

A large fish pulled the line and brought my expanse back into my petite, feminine form. The Captain wrestled the fish with strength and self-assurance. Once he pulled it into the boat, he said, "We'll eat well today." He put the large fish in its place and closed the lid. He washed his hands and sat next to me. In the peace and tranquility of the beauty and spaciousness all around us, he began to share stories about the sea, beyond his lifelong sport of surfing. The Captain, having grown up near the ocean had no fear of it and was even brave enough to get into the water at night. I was on the edge of my seat when he told me he went into the water to listen to the whales. He recorded their communication and played it for me on his digital device. It was amazing to hear their sounds. It gave me chills.

He did this in the dark. The whales would come to the surface and let him touch them. Their relationship had been going on for over three years. They would return to visit him when they would migrate back each year. He spoke about them like they were friends and family. The look in his eyes made it clear that his communing with them was truly a spiritual experience. I was touched by the way he became more vulnerable and open during his story telling. That drew me closer to him. I could tell that his time with the whales changed him. I do believe whales and dolphins are majestic creatures. I felt privileged to learn of his intimate encounters. The heart communicates without words in ways that lets us know that purity has spoken. I felt what spending time with whales did for him. It was through his heart that they touched me too.

The next thing I knew he was asking if I wanted to get into the water. Of course, I wanted to get into the water but I had to face my shark fears being so far out at sea. I could almost hear the Jaws soundtrack in my ears as I am imagined my limbs being chomped off. As I silently braced my fear, he dove right in without a second thought. I watched my constrictive breathing and scanned the surface for shark fins. Silently said, "F**k it" and dove right into my fear. The moment my body hit the water I witnessed both my mental and emotional body. One was communicating "A shark is going to bite your leg off," and the other was saying, "Ahh this water feels like heaven." The contradictory push and pull of creation are a fascinating experience. Over time, my mind had less control over my decision making. When I lived by fear my mind controlled my life. When my heart was in charge, I became fearless and clearer than ever.

My skin being very tactile feels highly stimulated by certain textures. The feeling of water against my skin has the ability to catapult me into a transcendence state. The soft, cool sensation of seawater feels like liquid love all over my body. How does water make you feel? Take a bath soon and answer that question for me. As for the ocean, I believe saltwater is healing and essential to my optimal well-being. It's a high-performance liquid elixir for my body consciousness. Diving into that pure blue water was the best decision I could have made. Fears exist but they aren't there to stop me, they are there for me to retrieve more of what my heart is after… freedom.

The Captain boned and filleted our fish when we got back onto the boat. After a mouthwatering lunch we motored off. The wind whipped my hair but not the smile off my face. It only grew wider in the sunlight that danced over the ocean surface. His next surprise made me squeal. He pulled up to the largest pod of dolphins I had ever seen in my life. I had been a scuba diver for ten years, while I was married, and had many dolphin encounters but not like this. He turned off the boat and I could hear the dolphins squealing, like I do. My jaw dropped. I could not believe the sea of dolphins before me. They were playing in the water and motoring along in a pod that seemed the size of a football field.

The Captain shouted, "Get in!"

My mind said, "What?" I love dolphins but hundreds of them!? Yikes! I was scared. He threw on a mask and snorkel and dove right in. "Oh shit!" I thought. Again, I had no time to dwell in my fear. I took a deep breath, grabbed the other snorkel and mask and dove in. Boy am I glad I did because it was an unbelievable experience. You may have no idea what it feels like to be in the middle of the ocean with a thousand dolphins, but I can say there's nothing like it. Dolphins are sonar creatures of the highest vibe, in my opinion. They were layered beneath me, beyond count. I had the fortunate experience to be a part of their pod, and made friends with a baby dolphin. He swam away from its mother and came right up to me. He looked directly into my eyes and seemed to smile at me. I laughed through my snorkel and observed how he did this several times, returning to his mother in-between his visits to me.

The Captain pulled his face out of the water and removed his snorkel to shout, "Play with him!"

I thought to myself, "What!?"

That's when I let the kid in me take over. One big, deep breath and downward I went, spiraling my body like I used to when I swam under the water in my grandmother's swimming pool as a kid. The baby dolphin mimicked me by spiraling his body! I had to come to the surface to giggle and to gasp for air. I went back down for more as we played together and spoke a universal language of joy. It was a sight to see and a memory that will remain in my heart forever.

I felt cleansed, clear and awakened when I got out of the water. You know that kind of squeaky-clean feeling that comes from the inside out? You can feel it on your skin and in your mind too. It was an energetic scrub that made me feel good all over. That's how I felt as we laughed and talked, and motored away to a new destination. Where the Captain made us another lovely grilled fish meal. The big, round, orange sun began to set. Turning the sky many shades of beautiful and putting an exclamation mark on an unforgettable day. I leaned back against his hard chest, feeling satisfaction in every cell of my body. He wrapped his strong arms around my waist. We fell into the sunset together. My heart was full of gratitude and a few tears of appreciation slipped down my face.

The Captain was a complete gentleman and didn't expect anything from me. He gave me a day of bliss and brought me back to my room 12 hours later. He hugged me and then looked into my eyes and asked if he could take me on a land adventure the following day. He said he needed to personally introduce me to Pele, the volcano. And there were a few other special places on the island I needed to see before I departed on Monday afternoon. I gave him a sweet, soft kiss on the lips and accepted his invitation. This time I didn't think it over. I just felt into the rightness of it. I drifted off to sleep that night pondering the unreal becoming real in my life. My old reality was washing away, one man, one land, and one breathe at a time. I was living more and more in a place of gratitude in the present moment. My courage to explore and to allow adventure, gave my innocence/purity an outlet to experience the freedom of feeling wildly alive.

The next day, when the Captain picked me up he mentioned a growing sparkle in my eyes. He was like an angel himself, who fed my sparkle more beauty and wonder. I was open to receiving more, which is an important act for the giver in us. Becoming limitless is about removing the limits we place on our current reality. I love to give and this man was helping me to be on the receiving end of all my giving.

It was a long drive to the volcano but worth the distance, as he had wonderful stories to share about living on the island. He spoke of a majestic and mysterious place called the goddess bath that was hard to find and quite hidden in the jungle. I myself was amazed to share with him that the first time I came to the island years prior, I was led to that bath and spent hours in it with a girlfriend of mine. The volcano was all new to me. I had never seen an active volcano in real life. When we arrived, it was amazing to see the steam coming out of its vast center. Like a cauldron of life breathing land into form. The earth was in her own primal contraction of creating life. A lava lake of bubbling earth took me into conscious breathing to feel the land being birthed. I was touched by what I saw and felt as nature made herself known - in me.

The black sand beach was our next stop. I had worn my swimsuit under my sundress and didn't think twice about whipping it off and tossing it on the sand and jumping in the water. My wild spirit was coming alive. The Captain didn't get a chance to warn me about the current. I was quickly whisked out to sea by a huge undertow. The ocean was like a vacuum, and my fear a bee, that stung me right out of my dream state. But the calm and capable Captain dove right in and managed to reach

200

me. His strong and steady presence guided me sideways out of the undercurrent and back towards the shore, in a different direction. The enormous power of the tide shocked me and almost swallowed me alive. It was a humbling experience to face the possibility of death at a moment's notice.

The Captain couldn't stop apologizing for not warning me. He didn't know I was going to jump in that quickly. That particular stop was about the black sand beach and the sea turtles. I didn't realize that until it was too late. The shocking experience led me to reflect and ask myself some important questions as we drove to the next destination. The Captain sat quietly giving me the space to go inward. I pondered the thoughts:

"Was I living my bliss? Was I happy with my life? If I could live anywhere, where would I live? If I could do anything, what would I do? What inspired me? How could I be of service to humanity? How could I leave this earth a better place than when I arrived?' "How could I be a guardian of the land and an inspiration for the people?"

These thoughts swirled in my mind, just like that undertow that almost took my life. When no one else could decide who I am, then who would I become? Those clarifying questions drew more of my heart out of me, and into the life I was consciously choosing to create. By surrendering to my highest and greatest potential I didn't know exactly what that would look like, but life was helping me to bring all of the lost and forgotten parts of me back, and into my physical form. Each new experience brought me new clarity, including being swept out to sea. Now that I was safe, I found myself considering, 'before I am done living, what am I living for?'

The car stopped at our final destination. I looked up to see a Tibetan temple surrounded by peacocks and palm trees. The Captain stepped out of the vehicle, bent down and picked up a peacock feather and handed it to me, like a flower. I thanked him as I waived it like a wand, while taking in the smell of incense, and the mysterious sounds of chanting, that were coming from the temple we were walking towards. The island was returning me to a dreamy, hypnotic state. My hips started to respond to the sounds I was hearing as music stimulates motion in my body.

I think dance is a healing modality that has also contributed to my transformation and well-being. My former identity of being shy, kept me from dancing until I freed myself from those chains of control. I've experienced a freedom and joy in dance and I understand why it's used in many cultures for ritual and celebration. As my hips swayed toward the temple, I waived my peacock feather in the air. The sweet motion, smells and sounds were raising my frequency to a higher vibration and I felt that in my body.

The feather was an appropriate take away that I brought home with me. The peacock absorbs light of certain wavelengths that lend to its iridescent glow. That very much felt like what my life experience was doing to me: altering my wavelengths, expanding my bandwidth, aligning me with the force of nature within me, and contributing to my glow.

The long drive back to the other side of the island that night, gave me time to sit with the many riches I received. When we got to my hotel, the Captain commented on how the sun and the moon shined on my face. This man knew how to make me smile, and I wanted to show him my appreciation for his priceless generosity. He never once pushed or forced himself on me, nor did he assume that for showing me the island I owed him anything. He gave unconditionally, generously and joyously. He genuinely wanted to get to know me, and to show me the magnificent island he called home.

I appreciated and respected him for all of the treasures he bestowed upon me, which included his gentle, yet strong and warrior-like, masculine nature. The alpha female in me was ever present to the gifts of affection I wanted to give to him. I wrapped my arms around his neck and pulled him close, got on my tiptoes and planted a long, wet, sensual kiss on his lips. It was instantly clear what that did to his body when he pulled me closer. I whispered an invitation in his ear asking him to come up to my room. He accepted.

This man was prepared for everything, including sex as I was pleasantly surprised that he carried a condom. Which I believe every man could be in the practice of. It's tough for women to insist because men like to say they are clean and that there's nothing to worry about. They have no way of proving that or accidentally impregnating us. That's a hefty weight to put on our shoulders. Be responsible men, and protect the women by putting on a condom without being asked.

The Captain impressed me with his compassion and consideration from start to end. He honored me, my space, my zest for adventure, and last but not least - my body. He took the time to get to know me. He used impulse control, even while I stood next to him for hours in a bathing suit. For the women who think men are supposed to jump their bones and rip their clothes off to show they like you, I prefer consensual sex with a man who is interested in wanting to get to know me first. That may only be a matter of hours or it could be days and weeks. There's a level of depth of connection that I appreciate. It comes from the heart. When I can feel that I open to more.

I was immediately attracted to The Captain when I first saw him. That was based only on his physical appearance, and the few kind things he said to me. After two full days with him, we had connected on all four levels: mental, emotional, spiritual and now it was time for a deeper level of the physical. When he got to my room I have to admit, all I wanted was to have our bodies merge. I wanted to feel him inside of me.

Once he knew I wanted him his sexual energy was tangible. However, he still didn't throw me down and force himself on me. He allowed me the privilege of slowly unbuttoning his shirt, like he was a present. My lips went right to his hard, tanned six-pack abs, kissing one muscle at a time. I had been quietly admiring his muscular form from the moment he pulled off his shirt on the boat. His body was like steel and his skin like copper. I could have stared at him naked for hours he was so sexy. He was even more appealing by the way he didn't flaunt it. I loved how well he took care of his body and wish every man offered up a well-maintained body. This man possessed kindness, consideration, good looks, a healthy body, forethought and impulse control, all of which required maturity and discipline. That made him hot on the inside and outside.

When his shorts dropped to the floor, I looked up at him and smiled in appreciation for his masculine form. I let myself enjoy every single part of him until he could no longer bare it. That was when he picked me up and laid me on the bed, slipped on a condom, and ever so gently entered me. I was wet and ready for him but I still needed the slow approach because it's intense to be entered, and far more enjoyable to feel the slow sensations of my own expansion, and his penetration. When a penis is immediately forced into me, it is either painful or numbing.

Baby's don't immediately come flying out of vagina and cocks should not go flying into one either. In my opinion, honoring the tunnel of creation and seeing it as a sacred center where our innocence and purity came into this world, is the way we can take sex to a whole new level. With that kind of appreciation, we honor life. Allowing sex to begin slowly and knowing things can change rhythm once we our expanded, is a way for us to better in touch with our feminine form. Impulse control is what will help keep men from just satisfying himself. Sex is about two bodies becoming One. By slowing things down ladies can have a chance to be more in touch with their own bodies, when it is not all about him. Ladies, notice if you just want him to get it over with because you don't enjoy it. Become aware. Part III is about tips I give to the men. You may want to read it too. However, that section called Sex & Balances will now be the start of my next book. This one went on longer than

I anticipated. I guess that means the next one will start out real juicy. Orgasms' are the beginning of that section.

Speaking of which, The Captains cock felt like a rod of electricity inside of me and that's not an exaggeration. It wasn't a painful spark but it was electric. Was it all the time he spent in the ocean surfing, boating, or with the whales? Was it that he lived his bliss and that I could feel his Inner Spark through his cock? Or was it our two bodies together that sparked the surge I felt inside of me? It was a current of energy that felt like buzzing electricity. The sensation made me open my eyes. I found him staring at me with this look of "Wow!' on his face. He could feel it too but neither one of us said anything.

We just smiled, laughed, and moaned with pleasure. It was unlike anything I had ever felt before. Other than a paranormal experience, I had in the River Jordan where my entire body felt like it was being electrocuted. However, this electricity was concentrated in one area, and it was inside of me. It seemed to vibrate all the way up into my womb like a hive of bees buzzing. It was a one-of-a-kind experience. The Captain truly left me speechless and beyond grateful for the time we spent together. His unexpected entry into my life and my pussy, resulted in me catching the first night, and the last morning of my weekend writing workshop. In the middle of my four-day weekend was content of my story... waiting to be told.

Chapter 23
Sunny

Months later, my inner exploration took me abroad once again. I landed on the Giza strip and began a 17-day journey that started at a sunrise ceremony at the Sphinx, and ended in a sarcophagus in the Great Pyramid, after sailing the Nile and touching down on many sacred sites throughout Egypt. I don't think that an inner exploration needs to take you to the places I have gone. By no means did I ever dream of going to these destinations. Your journey will be unique to you.

My life was shifting me from an outer authority, to a remembrance of an inner authority found in a relationship with my Higher Self. Which guided me in directions and in ways I never even imagined. It was a new practice and teaching that was distilling me; into the teacher, spokeswoman and leader I would become, on behalf of that guidance.

"I need a man and need to marry again," was a belief system with an engine that didn't just shut off. It was built upon generations passed down through lineages. Just like the control of the feminine and sexual shame. The same outer authority that shamed men for the purity in their hearts and didn't allow them to feel. I was willing to climb up out of that mountain of lies, to stand at its peak to reach out to each of you - to find your freedom too.

How I ended up in Egypt undergoing ancient initiations with a small group was as unbelievable to me, as it may seem to you upon reading this book. And yet, for some reason when the plane landed, I felt a part of me was returning home. That familiarity was something for me to discover as I awakened to the ancient within me.

For the conservative life I had led, my mystical travels were disorienting to my rational and idealistic mind, which was structured on concrete evidence, work ethic, and being like everybody else. I didn't know what Egypt had in store for me. But now I do, and all I will say is; be prepared when you go on a spiritual journey to Egypt because you'll never be the same again. Egypt was about quickening my learning, which felt more like a slap to my face about a month after I returned. It was one of the most intense transitions in my life, with the exception of my divorce that exploded my life like a bomb. The shrapnel I faced when my x-husband orchestrated hateful acts that removed: love, companionship, a child, homes, families, money, friends, work, neighbors (every sense of security and identity that brought me comfort) from my life.

Here I was, years later, having found footing in a new world of self-discovery not knowing Egypt was like receiving a doctorate in the mystical realms within me. That trip would command me to grow exponentially upon my return to reality. I didn't see that coming because I was on a high when I returned from Egypt. I felt so elevated I could see the future as if it were today. I didn't know that future was 5-10 years away.

What I learned first-hand is that the body takes time to integrate our light. While parts of my body awakened my mind had to process the misinformation consumed as truths and revealed as lies. No one explained this to me in school because they don't talk about evolution of our species and that by design, we awaken. I didn't realize the expansion of my consciousness stimulated parts of me I had long forgotten and could be a strain on my body. That our biology moves at a much slower pace than instant remembrance found in the heart. Integration was key.

While in the experience of the initiations in Egypt, I felt amazing as if my mind was expanding in all direction. In Peru, the initiations felt grounded and earthy. Where in Egypt they felt cosmic or celestial. While I was there, I enjoyed riding on camels and sailing the Nile. I felt I had stepped back in time, where everyone went to pyramids and temples, like we go to University for advanced education. The only difference was this schooling was about expanding our awareness by going within. The temples were designed to activate that remembrance where no one tells you what's true, you know truth through your Source connection found within.

The kicker was, I had to return to modern day life. Where I faced every unhealed experience, thought and belief when my Egyptian high wore off. That's when I felt the weight of the density I was carrying around like a busload of baggage. The years of personal work I had done paled in comparison to what was before me. I even had dreams of carrying more baggage than my hands could hold, and had to balance the rest on my head, which were piled high.

Egypt shed light on all of my unseen beliefs consumed as false narratives that lived as truth in my biology, until then. There was no gradual learning curve. It was abrupt. My mind was blown. You could say my ego was trying to hold on for dear life, to the little raft it was floating on. I faced sleepless nights and spiraled into a deep depression. How could such a high end in such a low? Well, when you shine a lot of light on someone, it can blind them. That's was me. What does this have to do with a man or men coming into my life? Well, a man, actually two of them, came into my life at this time.

The first one is unexplainable and mostly unbelievable. Nothing romantic happened but he did come to my aid and helped bring me back to life before he disappeared. He seemed like a real-life guardian angel and seemingly showed up out of nowhere. He lived in another state but would drive all the way to my house to get me out of bed. Let it be known, I'm not a lazy person. This was about depression and a lack of a will to live. That is how heavy I felt when all that was dark (unconscious) was fully illuminated. Raphael got me back to life and then was gone. I wrote about him in my first book, "Light me up!" by Andrea "Sis" Elliott found on Amazon.

The second man entered my life as a result of my former beliefs bullying me to fit-in with the rest of the world, insisting this faith and trust thing was B.S. That meant, I needed a full-time job immediately. I knew I wanted to help people move beyond their limited thinking and to reach for their highest and greatest potential but I was in my own larvae stage; a caterpillar becoming a butterfly. After spending months and years growing a peaceful mind, that had gotten used to living in the present moment, fear took over and held me hostage. I was forced by fear to become a sheep again. I knew how to work and I had been using that force for my own self-discovery, even if the outside world didn't see value in it. I was fully committed to living from the inside out. But my rational mind fueled by fear took control and convinced me I was going to die, starve and be poor if I didn't get a job right away.

I took on a social worker job. Being highly empathetic made my work very challenging. I dealt with people who were struggling with psychological problems, behavior disorders, and high levels of anxiety. Some of them felt numb and spaced out from their medications which was disorienting me. It was not a good choice of work for me but that was all I could find to help others, while dealing with my own disorientation. It was my social worker job that led me to the coffee shop in the middle of the afternoon, between clients, where Sunny spotted me. His wild hair and lively presence made him stand out. He was a character with a lot of heart but I had no interest in meeting a man or anyone, at that time.

Sunny approached my table and introduced himself as a painter, something else, and a candlestick maker. He got a kick out of himself and was on a mission to make himself known to me. I was not interested but that didn't stop him from chatting me up. I eventually apologized for being distant and unengaged, confessing I was moving through some emotional difficulties and wasn't good company at the time. He wanted to help me more than ever once he knew I was down and out. I politely excused myself but he insisted on walking me out and handed me his card saying, if I needed anything to call him. Even though he was a stranger, he was genuinely concerned about me. That's what heart will do.

There wasn't a chance I was going to call him and he probably sensed that and pushed for me to give him my number so that he could check up on me. I had little strength to resist his insistence and mumbled my number that he wrote on the back of a paint sample.

Eccentric Sunny ended up becoming my friend, who led me to the man I fell for next. It was Sunny's compassion and curious nature that brought him into my life. He had me over his house regularly and asked me questions about spirituality. Thankfully, his promptings brought out the spiritual teachings and practices in me, that had helped me transform. That was exactly the wisdom I needed to remember and hold onto through the major set-back I was experiencing. I had stopped my morning practice and intentions and wasn't feeling a closeness with my Higher Self during those months. Sunny's presence pushed me to be a better teacher and parent to myself, as I tuned back into my physical, spiritual and emotional needs, not just living from my shoulders up in my mental body only. An old and familiar habit I fell back into.

My mind had taken the opportunity to rape me while I was weak, and it succeeded in eliminating the magic and wonder in my life. Without the rest of me on board I was susceptible to being possessed by fear. Sunny was like a mother in a man's body, in the way he cared for me, which gave me the space to feel into my own heart again. I was able to dip back into the creative side of my brain to sense what felt right to me.

He would invite me over and cook for me. He would also make me healthy smoothies to nourish me. He even offered to wash my hair, more than once, as I was losing clumps of it from the inner war going on inside my mind that wanted to obsess on worry. It was all the parts of myself that I would need to die to, and they were holding on for dear life. One reboot at a time, was easier to handle than a cacophony of old programs running at once. I was in a crisis and the kindness of strangers helped me through. It was their aid that returned me to my spiritual practices and self-care regimen. My Higher Self knew how to lift me up but I needed to invite that wisdom in - to guide me again.

Sunny was another man who touched my life with his compassionate nature. His spiritual inquiry and nurturing presence helped me to remember my daily devotion to the wisdom within me. To drive my high-performance vehicle, I needed to remember daily maintenance. Perseverance was the oil that greased that engine; an unwavering commitment to honoring my Higher Self. That is how I returned to the present moment again.

When my years of spiritual studies were resourced through me, for the sake of Sunny's curiosity, I resumed my 'student of life' status and was pushed to be the natural teacher I was becoming. The relationship with my spiritual nature was accessed in my mental body. His openness, curiosity, generosity and nurturing presence also supported my emotional and physical body. I was set back into motion when all four tires of my high-performance vehicle were engaged again. My spiritual body was in development and all four tires needed balancing.

Sunny brought me gifts from his heart that touched my life. We became close friends when he cared for me the way a brother cares for a sister. Having been very close to my brother when I was young, for those few months, Sunny became the brother I needed. His care and compassion helped me to heal. He was also the bridge to my next lover and life lesson.

Chapter 24
Dream Man

Personal growth means we discover patterns that allow us to create change in our lives. Months later, I was swept into one of my main patterns and I didn't do so well. I was more invested in my unconscious habits, beliefs, and codependency patterns than I had realized. My next lesson began to take shape when Sunny invited me to a party, where I met an old acquaintance of his. A man I fell for the moment I laid eyes on him. This was the man I would marry and we would live happily ever after. I got sucked right back into my school girl brainwashing moments after we said hello to one another.

Dream Man had a close relationship with his parents and two brothers. All of which I met soon after we began dating. I know, I know, you may just want to hear about the sex. Well, let me tell you, I appreciated his amazing body and gorgeous face when I met him. When I saw him naked almost two months later, I wanted him even more. But there were complications. His rugged but well-groomed look turned me on so much, I could have made love to him every day. Women don't always get the chance to have smarts, grounded success, dependability, perfect height, a gorgeous face and hot body all wrapped into one man. This is what made him my Dream Man.

I respected his profession, family and the home he had built with his own two hands. But as you know, there's the spiritual and emotional that go along with the package. He had the mental body that intrigued me and a face and physical stature, I wanted to look at and touch for the rest of my life. Although he was ruggedly handsome, I couldn't just have him when I wanted to because of underlying issues that made their way into the bedroom. There were emotional issues that led to his sexual hang-ups, prohibiting us from having sex as often as I would have liked. I was baffled and didn't know what was going on. I resorted to silently blaming myself, as he kept his issues to himself.

Unlike me, who was introspective and willing to look at my hang-ups and limitations, he was walled in, controlled, and protective of his vulnerable and unseen areas. He wasn't on a blazing path of self-realization like I was at the time. He was however, just learning to meditate and would "sit" in a Buddhist practice, alone or in a group once a week. He hid his alcoholism and smoking from me, while simultaneously bringing me closer to him and his family. We would have dinners with them each week, and he'd invite me to spend nights sleeping over his house. That's how I continued playing house and 'happily ever after' in my mind.

Since I was falling for him the moment, he said hello, I was trying to understand why he didn't find me as sexually desirable as I found him. Of course, we never talked about it openly. I remained confused when I felt and saw him get excited. It was obvious we turned each other on but then he seemed to push me away, at the same time he pulled me closer. Something was off.

We continued dating and introducing one another to our friends. We joined the same gym. I didn't hide my affection for him. I was becoming bolder and had no problem showing

216

everyone I adored him. But there was a wall we kept hitting because of his undisclosed issues. I tried to figure it out on my own. It had to be me. Blaming myself for disharmony was something I had learned to do well as a child.

There was another component that had to do with his mother. I noticed the huge influence she had over him, and how she seemed to be the only one in the family who wasn't warm and open with me. I'm a friendly and considerate person and did everything I could to show her respect. But she still made him weary of me and made him question himself. In fact, he would ask me strange questions that he would later tell me they came from his mother. There was that, and there was more. And eventually I got it all. Not him. But, the story behind the issue.

It took months to discover the obstacle and it came out after Dream Man had one too many drinks. He confessed that his Dad had run a brothel when he was a young boy. When his mother would bring him to go see his father, who had an office in the house where the women worked, his mother would cover his eyes and pull him toward her. She didn't want him to see the pretty girls in lingerie. They were naughty or the represented something that was bad.

I could hardly believe that a brothel was in operation in his childhood, or that his family was business in that business, but that's beside the point. Even more interesting was how it impacted him as a boy. When his mother would grab him, cover his eyes and pull him away to "protect" him; those sexy ladies became marked in his psyche as something negative. That was valuable information for me because it explained why he shut down when I'd take off my clothes. Here I was, the sexy lady in lingerie. His excitement would shift when my lingerie was exposed. I couldn't understand why he'd look away or leave the room when I took off my shirt or pants. My lacy panties and bras represented something he needed to be protected from. An old program still running in his mind as a grown man was getting in the way of us enjoying each other's bodies more. It then made sense to me why his former wife of over 20 years wasn't a cute or petite woman. She didn't fit the profile of someone sexy, but I did.

Unbeknownst to me, I was triggering him every time we got intimate. When I undressed in front of him, he shut down. This explained why he started asking me to meet him under the covers. When he did that a part of me felt rejected. I had grown to love my body, and I adored my pretty, lacy undergarments. Being female is a joy and I didn't think of hiding my beauty as I was just finding comfort in it. However, my people-pleasing habits were quick to get on board. Whatever he wanted and would make him happy, even if sex would remain missionary style, under the covers only, I could do that for him.

I wanted to enjoy so much more with Dream Man for years to come but it wasn't a dream that would become a reality. He was new on the path of self-awareness and wasn't willing to go into his discomfort or to even talk about it again. Life was teaching me detachment and to unconditionally love myself, even when others rejected me. The complete opposite of codependency was a brutally tough lesson for me to learn. Dream Man was my temptation and I fell for him hard. I loved cooking meals together and having dinners with his family. I had lost more than one family. With him, I had one again, and a man with looks that took my breath away. Even if his mom didn't love me, I loved all of them. I was willing to give anything of myself to be with him. There was clear chemistry but he was not emotionally, fully physically, or spiritually available to me. I would have waited it out putting myself last for as long as I needed to but he wasn't up for the growth. I was ready to sacrifice myself as a habit but detachment was forced on me, when he broke up as he became more triggered, trying to stuff what was coming up to be healed.

He wouldn't talk about his fears to move beyond them. Once he was sober, his wall went back up and it seemed tougher than ever. It almost seemed like he resented me for having shared his vulnerability with me. He became less kind as the pain of the past surfaced to be healed. How dare I bring out his softness is what the chip on his shoulder said to me. It positioned me like a villain of sorts, at the end. I was the one to blame. It was my fault he felt discomfort. The loss of control he felt in his vulnerability was managed through anger and resentment he misdirected toward me. I was the one who shined light on his pain but it wasn't my fault or my issue. It was an opportunity for him to heal.

I had not seen the mean and angry side of him in the first 3 or 4 months we were together. The emotions that were under the anger weren't something he wanted to deal with so he went toward the only emotion he found acceptable. The macho man, who doesn't show vulnerability and who forgets he's made of innocence, went back into his man box. I then reverted to my martyrdom, people-pleasing female box and tried to please him with kindness. I never expressed my sexual needs and quietly settled for whatever he was willing to give or not give. What Dream Man represented was the life that society deemed acceptable: hide your issues, mask them with addictions and denial, let rage simmer in the background, and play happy in public.

I did bring out fun parts of his inner child that I'm sure other women had not seen in him. He loved my playful nature and would enjoy chasing me around the house. Which was a big deal for Mr. Macho letting himself have fun. I loved that playful kid in him. Our relationship was an example of unhealed traumas and old beliefs that stood in the way of deeper intimacy. I was willing to take the time necessary for him to come to terms with his stuff as I know it's a process. For me, I had my own people-pleasing and "blame it all on me" issues to heal, as well.

I adored him and I showed him that in every way imaginable. I was willing to stand with him in his self-discovery but he wasn't willing to go there himself. The alcohol and anger was the companion he chose over me. It broke my heart when he broke up with me. I bought into the "happily ever after" dream in my mind and believed I needed a man to complete me. I thought he was "the one" and cried my eyes out when it was over.

I had my codependent issues to heal, by becoming more aware of my part in it all. I was again forced to learn to love myself, even when someone else could not love me. Life was teaching me hard lessons of non-attachment that my once co-dependent nature in a relationship was very resistant to learning. Thankfully, I was willing to take an honest look at myself and each experience helped me do just that. Even if it wasn't in the moment, I was able to reflect afterwards to see what pieces were in there for me to heal. What programs I could delete and what new ones I could download.

The new was showing me the old. When I fell back and obeyed habitual ways, I could see how I sacrificed my self-love, spiritual knowledge or overlooked my instincts. In reflection, I could see how I let habits win because they were so convincing, familiar and comfortable. I was used to burning my steak to sacrifice my heart. Thankfully, I eventually could smell the burn of my convincing mind. I was willing to go into the burn to rescue the most precious and invincible part of me. That took the bravery of loving myself unconditionally.

I was growing my muscle of awareness and it did make me sweat, because my mind was firmly gripped to one reality. Flexing that muscle also made me cry as my heart was broken, over and over again. There was a balance I had not yet achieved but I was a work in progress and willing to do the work on myself. I was laying an emotional and spiritual foundation in my life that required my continued commitment because with it; I gained confidence and clarity. I was working towards designing my life where I honored myself and life itself - as a daily practice.

Once I was over my breakup with Dream Man, I was more solid in a commitment to my: mind, heart and body awareness. I had far more growing to do. I did so by delving into more books, self-growth workshops and international conferences on human understanding. At my next conference, I found that Brazil had a teaching waiting for me, in the form of a heart surgeon.

Chapter 25
A Taste of Brazil

The next man who gave me a new perspective on sexuality, left a lasting impression on me, in northern Brazil. For a woman who had never traveled alone, some of my lessons had me panning the globe - solo. Loosening my grip on co-dependency and opening me up to new and unexplored possibilities. The last speaker at the Parapsychology conference I was attending was a cardiologist, who had me almost jumping out of my skin, in a full-body 'yes!' to his research findings based on the heart. He was expounding on the heart being a center of guidance, wiser than the brain, and perhaps the real knowledge that we seek. I knew what he was saying was true. Although, I didn't have the data to prove it like he did. I was living in the 'knowing' of his research and that is why I was ecstatic that he had proof of heart intelligence. The brain was always receiving credit. The heart had finally received the spotlight.

I was so inspired that I leaped out of my seat, when he finished his talk, and walked directly up to him. My thoughts and enthusiasm shot out of my mouth as I approached him. At the very same time a man, from another direction, arrived by his side. The message I had arising from within me was being heard by me, as I was saying it. It was a beautiful message and it touched me.

After sharing my enthusiasm, in the form of a channeled message, the doctor pulled me aside. He politely apologized to the man who was waiting to speak to him and proceeded to lecture me on social mannerisms of Brazil. Which did not cater to empowered western women. He told me that in his country it was most respectful to let a man speak first and that I should have waited. The doctor was a tall, fiery, and confident man. I thought he was pulling me aside to thank me for what we both just heard. I was obviously wrong. Instead, he thought it was appropriate to give me a time-out. He held my upper arm as he spoke to me. Driving home his patriarchal dominance and authority over me. I respectfully listened and apologized for my lack of social grace. I then innocently giggled and surprised myself by saying, "Even knowing this, I still would have spoken up because the message wasn't about me. It was relevant to your work." His need to dominate and control the situation burnt the steak of the message I delivered. It didn't however, extinguish my own Source connection. The growing affection for my own heart, and my ability to take healthy control over my own self made a difference.

It felt good in my body to stand for my loving, clear heart. Today, I would have taken things further, by making it clear to him that his grip on my arm was unacceptable to my body. No matter what country I was in, that wasn't okay. But at that time, the embodiment of my own power was something I felt and experienced when I made it clear I was not rolling over and just taking it. That took practice. My new experience gave me an unexpected opportunity to do just that. I was willing to face a powerful man and feel uncomfortable for a moment, to feel more comfortable in the affection of my own heart. When I did speak up for myself the doctor seemed to appreciate my playful and bold nature.

The next thing I knew, he was the one approaching me, in the lobby as I headed out for dinner. He invited me to join him and suggested a restaurant that he knew. I accepted and we had a fun and lively conversation. I never expected to end up in bed with him later that night but that's exactly what happened. Our intellects were dancing in delight over the delicacies we shared during our meal. Our bodies naturally wanted to merge to explore more. There was a comfort and a magnetism between the two of us, but I had no intention of sex. He, on the other hand, did.

Here was another new sexual experience waiting for me, in an unexplored land far, far away from my normal reality. His strength of mind and personality was as tough as a bull. At any other given time in my life, I would have been intimidated and shy. But not the new woman I was becoming. I was intrigued and curious. That openness led me to learn more about men, my body, and the power of orgasm.

His six-foot frame seemed to devour me the moment the hotel door closed. He was strong and yet surprisingly tender in the way he approached my body and undressed me. I liked seeing his softer side, as his aggressive nature was ever present from the moment we met. My body liked the way that he touched me, and the way that he kissed me. There was a care and consideration in his approach. My conditioned mind did try to distract me with shameful thoughts that paid homage to virginal ways. Simultaneously, my growing awareness overcame those thoughts and allowed me the space to be in the experience of enjoying the pleasure of it all.

The sensual force of Mr. Brazil was intense. He showed me how far unbridled passion could go. He ravished my flesh one slow kiss at a time, as if I were dessert. After putting on a condom, he entered me with his throbbing hard cock, one slow inch at a time. That slow, hot, snug entry was more like a countdown to a rocket launch, that anyone within a mile radius could have heard when it exploded. I had never witnessed a man discharging with that level of volume in all my life. With no shame, inhibition, or sexual baggage this man verbally let loose a moan as if he had been shot. I was surprised the police didn't come to the door. It was that loud and painful sounding. The visual of his ecstatic release was equally as dramatic as his body spasmed. It made me wonder if his orgasm was more natural in its expression than the common squelching of an orgasm, with little to no sound or movement I was used to.

Are people in the habit of caring too much about what other people think of them? Is it that, as one string of a shoe lace, combined with unconscious sexual shame being the other lace, looped together as a perfect little bow of disconnect with our own bodies? Do we not feel permitted to be so vulnerable and authentic in expressing our emotional body when we release into ecstasy?

Now I knew what was possible when there's no holding back. It was amazing to see the power of an orgasm without denial, shame, and control. Mr. Brazil upped the primal energy bar by displaying the power packed in an orgasm and just how therapeutic and freeing it can be. The letting go and surrender of it all without trying to regain immediate composure seemed more natural and healing. I don't see surrender as being an act of doing nothing, but a movement into something more.

Was it his acceptance of his emotional body that allowed him to experience such heights of pleasure? I never saw anything like it, before or after. Until many years later, when I witnessed a wail and a tremble from a lover that convinced me he was having a seizure. Afterwards, he confessed he had not had an orgasm that intense before so it wasn't his normal. But in both instances, these men didn't try to control their body's natural release. Quite frankly, I found men who could let themselves be that vulnerable brought something uniquely special to lovemaking.

Mr. Brazil even inspired me around the feeling and expression of my own orgasm. We know that not everyone can bring us to such heights but those who can will never fault us for expressing how good it feels. I appreciated and respected both of these men's capacity to feel and to express. Although I didn't have an orgasm with Mr. Brazil, he did get extra points for consensual sex, as he respectfully asked me for what he wanted when we got to my room. I did not feel pressured or forced in any way. Our time at dinner sealed our mental and spiritual connection through great conversation. That led to our physical and emotional bonding later that night. Up until a Taste of Brazil, I had not realized just how contained we are, as a people, around our sexual joy. Not everyone is mired in sexual hang-ups. But, a vast majority of us have room to grow. My very unexpected sexual encounters were giving me the space to grow. I share what I have learned to inspire a society free of shaming men's feelings and women's bodies. I believe we can create a healthier society by learning to accept our Source connection, our feelings, and that wisdom in our bodies.

Chapter 26
Workshop Transformation

After Brazil, I attended workshops in Arizona on sexuality and one in Seattle on personal mythology. I didn't have sex at the sexuality conference but I did meet a very sexy woman (and no I don't sleep with women but I do appreciate beauty) who spoke at the conference. I was fascinated by her polyamorous relationship with the two men she was traveling with and committed to. She had a baby with one of them but all three of them lived together. It blew my mind. It wasn't a lifestyle for me but I was still intrigued by her strength, beauty and confidence to live outside of the box. She was a sex therapist who was highly educated about the physical body and spoke about topics related to sex and intimacy. I learned a lot in that weekend.

Interestingly, when I moved to California, I ran into her in the locker room of a high-end gym. A month later I ran into her again when I attended a friend's party. She pulled up next to me as I got out of my car. It turned out she lived next door. She thought the coincidences were uncanny and asked if I would be open to doing an interview with her at her home later that month. That same kind of serendipity continued in my life the more I opened to my Higher Kingdom. The unreal became real, as those two were an equal blend of a higher frequency of living, that was becoming my new normal.

The workshops and conferences I attended grew my network of scholarly, conscious connections. Many of which were leaders, doctors, and influencers in the area of consciousness.

These new people quenched my thirst for knowledge and inner expansion. Their depth of connection and deep understanding of life and themselves made life far more interesting. I was able to dive deeper within myself by being in the company of extremely intelligent and consciously aware people. I was also returning to an area of interest that continuously took me out of the ordinary and into the explorer of the human potential.

My workshop in Seattle brought a temporary mentor into my life. He was an older professor who had designed the personal mythology workshop I was attending. The revelations that came out of that workshop blew my mind. He had us do some simple but profound exercises of stepping into the people who had raised us, and then speaking as them. That exercise in particular allowed me to become clearer around the unconscious messages I was still working to gain sight of. Over that entire weekend we explored the mind, body and spirit in the most unique ways, that propelled more healing and growth for me.

The workshops and conferences also centered and focused me on what mattered most to me - my human potential. I was a student and a scribe of my own transformation and change. Those writings would eventually evolve into my books, and serve as teachings for me and others to face fears and to learn choice is a life of sovereignty. My learning continued outside of the workshop when I headed to my room one evening.

I was staying on the university grounds, when a group of men in their mid-20's befriended me. They invited me back to their room where we chatted for a little while before I headed to my room on campus. One of the young men, who I connected with most, asked if he could walk me to my room. I accepted his invite and we enjoyed each other's company for an hour or two when we got back to my room. We did not have intercourse but we did enjoy making out like teenagers. He was taking acupuncture and eastern medicine courses that we both enjoyed talking about. I was using acupuncture and homeopathy to support my body's transformation. His understanding of the meridians and the body's natural healing abilities made for a deep and interesting talk. You could say we were both a welcomed and unexpected surprise in each other's lives that evening. He was delightful and so many ways.

The workshops I was investing in challenged me to face more fears. One of my big fears was speaking up, or even talking with other people in a large group. When all of the attention was placed on me, I would feel heat and pain in my body. That had been an issue for me since childhood. My voice and my sensitive nature were met with physical force and verbal insults as a child. The habits of being invisible and remaining silent were more of a problem for me as an adult. When I did speak, my entire body went through a flush of adrenaline. It was quite painful. My body would heat up and my face and neck would turn bright red.

I had many moments when I was free of that past issue but it wasn't gone yet. The workshops I attended required full participation. Therefore, I was challenged to deal with this painful issue. The worst was when we went around their room and I had to wait until it was my turn to speak. The anxiety would mount. I could barely heart anyone else because I feared when it would be my turn to speak. Since we were there to address and face our issues and to talk openly about them, I not only had to

231

deal with the physical discomfort I had to push the fear out into the center of the group for all to see it, with me.

Needless to say, spending time with the sweet man I met in the residence hall was a playful diversion and a nice way to integrate my personal work. Giggling and chatting with him about Eastern medicine allowed my playful nature the space to enjoy my interests in alternative medicine, men and my body. The unexpected variety of men who entered my life were allowing me to sample new and unique experiences that; delighted my mind, body and heart. It also taught me detachment as the "marriage message" planted in my psyche as a child, wasn't necessarily something I was after the more I got to know myself.

On my last day of the personal mythology workshop, the professor called me Aurora Borealis, and then pulled me aside and said, "You have something important to communicate to the world. You have a unique way of seeing life. Your perspectives and perceptions need to be heard. If you don't have a Master's degree get one so that you will be taken seriously. That's just how the world works. Advanced degrees are required for legitimacy."

What? I had no plans on going back to school for my master's degree. The school of hard knocks was already giving me a degree in "overcoming obstacles." Now more was expected of me? It seemed like a lot to take in but it did feel good to be seen in such a significant way. My workshop was full of scholarly people and executives. In fact, he said most of the attendees were doctorates.

On the following Monday, the professor sent me an email saying he had over 1800 emails to reply to when he got back to his office, but that he was writing to me first because he meant what he had said. Wow! That stood out to me. He said he wanted to support my step toward getting my next degree. I was cc'd on his following email that had a recommendation letter attached to it. He had written directly to the president of a university on the Big Island recommending me as a student in their science department. Returning to school for my Master's Degree in Science was set into motion at that moment. It came with the other bold step I was taking to finally make my move to California. My attempt three years prior was sidetracked but now I had the inner resources to redirect my life.

I had already put my home on the market at the start of that year but there was no movement on it whatsoever, thanks to "The Big Short" mortgage scheme. It wasn't labeled as such at that time but the pain of it was being seen as home prices plummeted and jobs were lost. It was the worst time to sell but it was time for me to move on. I followed instincts and have now been in the practice of living without my nest egg ever since. Money stopped controlling my life when I freed myself from its matrix of control.

The other thing that happened upon my return from the workshop, was an introduction to a man who asked me if I would speak at a large prison to inspire the inmates. He had a connection to the prison system and felt I was a woman of inspiration and that I could influence the men. Without a second thought, I agreed and weeks later with no script in hand, I stood before hundreds of men, who were lifers. It was a moving experience on so many levels.

The once terrifyingly shy girl inside of me, no longer felt unsafe in my body. The more I cleared out the baggage of the past, (old beliefs, ideals, and habits) the more life lined-up for me, to be of service in ways that allowed me to inspire, guide and teach through my life experience. Sharing my insights and acquired knowledge felt good. At that prison talk, I watched tough, grown men cry in my presence and give me a standing ovation. Many of them wrote to me for months afterwards. I so appreciated all of their letters and the opportunity to be a healing influence in their lives.

Life was putting me into my role. It wasn't something I had to force, it was the woman I was becoming as my highest and greatest potential. That was the woman in me who was connected to Source. My job was to allow, listen, heal, breathe, surrender, intend and to follow my heart. Not listen to the dictates of others but to myself. Life challenged me to become more balanced in both the masculine and feminine aspects within me. That required a balance of mind and heart. I needed to listen to my heart more but my mind was as necessary in helping me to establish firm boundaries and to clearly state my needs.

It was the last four months of this particular year of great learning, where I had signed up for a final workshop, all the way down in San Diego. The idea came to me to find my new home in California on my return from that workshop. I decided to give myself 10 days to find a rental before returning back to my current home. I was so certain about the move, even without one offer on my home, I decided I would leave my car in LA, and fly back to pack my home. I scheduled a certain amount of footage in a semi as the most affordable means of moving my belongings. I would have two days to load it myself before it was picked up. It turned out that Mr. B.C. would come across the border to help pack my things. I trusted my heart and the process and felt certain about living in California by the end of the year. I went ahead and moved forward with each step, despite no proof that my home would sell.

Call it crazy to live with that kind of faith and trust but it all worked out. Interestingly, that wasn't even the most outrageous part of my fourth quarter plan. Before you judge me, let it be known that I've never paid a bill late and to this day, I have one of the highest credit scores achievable. Without a limitless budget, my house having not had one offer in a year's time while lowering the price three times, I decided to cruise the Mediterranean before making my way to California. What?! I know, I know! I can hardly believe I would have done something that outrageous myself. It blew my mind too.

The trip came out of left field and landed on my lap via a wrong number. The woman from the cruise line was confirming a date change. It was a miscall, that led to her giving me a deal of a lifetime to cruise the Mediterranean on an Italian speaking cruise ship. I do not know how I remained as cool as a cucumber trusting and accepting the unexpected. Those three months of my life could be made into a movie because no one could have written the script. I'll tell you about all of the men I met on that voyage abroad in the next chapter. And as the last segment of "The Men."

In the meantime, on the other side of the cruise, I drove down to California, ended up making friends with a woman at my San Diego workshop, who serendipitously lived in the town I was planning on moving to in LA county. She offered me her spare bedroom and said I could stay with her while I looked for my new home. Thanks to her kindness and the support of the universe I found a place. Can you believe my new home came to me though a friend who I had met in Egypt? She happened to think of me while I was in Los Angeles. I told her I was in California looking for a place to live. Moments later she forwarded me an email with the words, "This is your new home" in the subject line. I had found two places I was considering at that point but when I went to look at the place she sent to me - it was perfect. Even crazier, the home was right across the street from the home of the woman I was staying with! She is still a close friend of mine today. Alignment with my heart brewed up miracles in my life that even shocked me. The heart is where that magic lies.

My mind would never have imaged that a sublet, not publicly advertised and directly across the street from where I was staying, would become my new home. My mind also didn't imagine that a new friend from my personal mythology workshop, who lived in Seattle, would offer me his spare car for when I returned to pack making it possible to leave my car in California. When I flew back to Seattle, he kindly picked me up and drove me back to his house to borrow his car for my final three weeks of living up North. I went home and began packing. By chance Mr. B.C. made contact with me and offered to help me pack. As the two of us were loading the container outside of my home, a couple pulled up and asked if my home was still for sale.

The for-sale sign had been taken down a day or two before because my contract was up with the agent. The new friend who lent me his car had told his friends about my home. They showed up at the eleventh hour and made me an offer. The husband handed me a rose petal rosary, he had handmade and was in a heart shaped box with an angle on the lid. He said, "Will you accept this as our commitment until we get the deposit check next week?" I was speechless on how all of this was playing out. I agreed to his offer. We signed a contract within days of my departure and by the end of the following month, we closed on my home. First you perceive, then the universe conspires in your favor to create that perception. Once creation took form, I saw the miracle of it with my own eyes. I lived it over and over again. I know how it works.

The new version of me - directed by my Higher Self was nothing like the shy, indecisive, worried about pleasing others and fitting in, living in the past, worried about the future, old me. I had arrived at the present moment and was living there more and more. I was constantly given tests, as opportunities to choose faith and trust, over habit and doubt. There was a Joan of Arc fearlessness that continued to rise in me. I didn't even know that part of me existed, until I passed the tests that the universe sent my way. I learned to shed the fears of deeming "force" was bad as I embraced it within me. My connection with my heart or my Inner Spark was a beacon of light. It was my Spirit that knew I was safe, protected, guided and provided for - every day and in every way.

When I didn't seek outer approval or anyone's permission, my life opened up like the Great Sea parting. In that parting, before I moved to California, I got the idea to visit some of my new international friends, before, during and after my unexpected cruise along the Mediterranean Sea. This next adventure was not led by an organized group, and had nothing to do with a conference or a workshop. This was me choosing to go and do what I wanted. Although the ship had its destinations, I was on my own. It was me and my adventurous spirit on a journey of a lifetime. My great awakening had a purpose with hidden pleasures and treasures all along the way. I just had to be bold enough to claim them for myself.

The universe never tells us what to do because we are free. These next three chapters were about me choosing and making my own decisions. It wasn't about being told the answers by somebody else. It was about living life beyond pain and difficulty, by grabbing life by the balls, and claiming my own sense of adventure, in ways I never dreamed possible. I'm all for structure and for going with gut instincts. In order to balance both, I had to first tip the scales toward going with my instincts/feelings. That is what allowed me to sample the varieties of life, which better informed me of my rich and diverse character. Grab your passports and your imagination, and join me on my adventure of a lifetime.

Chapter 27
All Aboard

London

The first leg of my journey was to London to visit a friend I had met in Peru. He was an attorney who grew up in England. I met him at a time in his life he was moving more into his multidimensional self as was I. I stayed at his flat and took a day trip to Glastonbury and Stonehenge. I loved the lush, green terrain, the gnomes, leprechauns, and sprite-filled air that seemed to dance all around me, as I explored the shops of Glastonbury. Stonehenge had its own air of mystery in a portal kind of way but it didn't catapult me into the fairy realms quite like Glastonbury. The start of my trip did stir a well of magic inside of me. The mystery within was awakened to come out and play.

I flew to Genoa Italy three days later to board my Italian speaking cruise ship. It was a very unusual way that my trip came to be. There's no doubt in my mind that had I not spontaneously committed right there and then; I would have never taken the trip. I pulled together my additional itinerary after confirming with my friends who lived abroad. My last night was spent with a stranger through a website called couchsurfing.com. There is no sexual encounter to report on that last night of my trip. But it's worth mentioning that following my heart led to us becoming friends. We ended up meeting back up a year later in the Canary Islands. She had me stay as her guest during her summer vacation. I could have never dreamed any of this up as my story wrote itself. My job was to take one step at a time, and to allow things to unfold in the present moment. The new me was fearlessly boarding planes, making diverse friendships and straddling continents without hesitation. My Higher Self didn't operate in the constraints of fear-based thinking or habits tied to lack and limitation.

Genoa

When I landed in Genoa, I discovered I was a day early for the cruise. Yikes! It was how they wrote dates in Europe that threw me off. My mistake made me freeze in fear and blurt out my shock right there on the street corner. I was all ready to board the ship and was standing at the corner where the line should have been forming. There was no line, and no ship. That was when my new South African friend made himself to me. He happened to be standing on that corner when I smacked my head in disbelief, discovering the juxtaposition of the day and month on my boarding pass.

My new state of living in the present moment was gruffly disrupted by a barrage of fearful judgments that pummeled me for my mistake. It's amazing how clear the voice of judgment is when it's not been around 24/7 anymore. Not only were the once silent and unconscious thoughts in my mind now heard, the sensations of fear were equally identifiable. My body felt like someone hit the switch of anxiety. It was direct assault to my nervous system. I had gotten used to going with the flow, feeling peace and satisfaction more each day. When fear returned, a distinguishing sensation of contraction came with it.

I had already crossed an earlier hurdle of dealing with my two oversized bags getting lost on my flight to London. They showed up three days late and just minutes before my departure to Genoa. I dealt with that inconvenience and with the worry of what I would do if they didn't show up before my two-week cruise. Those enormous bags, resembling all of the baggage I was letting go of, taught me a great lesson - to never overpack again! But at that time, I was still carrying the baggage. And, at that moment they were parked on either side of me. In a foreign land... destination unknown.

The kindness of strangers constantly blessed by life. This time it was in the form of Mr. South Africa who made things better. He was a kind, gentle and generous businessman - become angel. He immediately expressed empathy and a willingness to help me. He offered to take me to lunch and to help carry my bags, until I sorted things out. That was so helpful. I was in one of those moments where I couldn't think straight because fear had its way with me. In other words, I needed to breathe. His nurturing presence was just what I needed, and it was the last thing I expected.

Mr. South Africa was in Genoa on business and knew the town well. I accepted his warm invite and hours later we were chatting away like two long lost friends. He was open and vulnerable. He told me about his fiancé and how nervous he was about their marriage upon his return. Those were valid feelings for anyone about to get married. I was happy to be of emotional support to him, as he was the same for me. At the end of our meal, he offered his room as a place to stash my bags to take me on a tour of the city. When we got to his large European hotel room, he pointed across the room at the bed just under the picture window overlooking the courtyard. He said I could sleep there if I wanted to. He had his own larger bed on the other side of the room. Just having a place to store my bags was a huge relief. I thanked him for the offer and let him know I would think about it. His compassion and care went a long way. I can't even begin to explain what an honest, non-threatening man offers a woman in distress. I felt protected and safe in a foreign land, thanks to his kindness and care.

My extra 24-hour window was a test for me to pass without judgment. It would have been easy to get down on myself, out of habit. Instead, I restored my peace with self-forgiveness and through accepting an act of kindness from a stranger. That resulted in me making a new friend and learning about a new city. I was brave enough to travel alone but that didn't mean I didn't have to face fear. Becoming fearless required facing fear. With it, came rewards. In this situation, it was a caring man who massaged my heart with his actions. A city I would have passed through without a second thought, treated me to two great meals, a guided tour, a mini shopping spree, and the most enjoyable company I could have ever imagined. Andrea was bright, charming, and well-traveled. Strangely enough, we had the same first name. In some parts of the world, Andrea is a man's name.

The morning after our sleepover, I thanked my new friend for sharing his room and vulnerabilities concerning his engagement with me. I learned a lot about him, his profession, and the woman he loved. We had created trust in the time we spent together the day before. That made it easy for us to share a room together.

We continued to stay in touch via social media when I made my way onto that social platform. He's now a proud father and seems to look fulfilled in his new role. His natural doubts about tying the knot are an example of how our brains question the desires of our hearts. We may also question what's come before because it doesn't work for us. Either way, that leads us to the unknown. That's not an easy place to put trust but with practice what seems scary can bring us something totally new.

That's was what I was walking into, when I left my new friend and headed for my cruise ship the following day. It still amazes me how I was able to surrender to the entire experience. From spending the money, to traveling on planes, trains, and a huge ship; visiting over a dozen cities and exploring eight countries all alone. I grew up believing I'd live in the same town for the rest of my life. I lived an ordinary and uneventful life. Other than my parent's emotional rollercoaster of constant fighting, dinner was at 5pm, and church was every Sunday. The only family vacation we took, once a year, was by car to visit my grandparents who lived two states away. When I got married, we did travel to his chosen destinations, but it still didn't prepare me for my mind-altering journey of self-discovery.

Welcome to My Cabin

You're probably wondering about the sex because it's been a while, but don't worry it's coming. Even though I had no idea at the time. When the shipped pushed off for our first stop in Naples I was happily unpacking my oversized suitcases in my cozy cabin. I loved how snuggly it felt in my own room. I had been on a couple of cruises when I was married. Alaska was a favorite. but having the whole room to myself felt amazing. I liked it far better than sharing my room as it sparked the realization that I value having my own sleeping space to myself. A traditional role with couples having to share the same bedroom wasn't necessarily for me. But I had never considered another possibility until that moment. I never slept well next to my husband. The years I spent outside my marriage helped me to discover that I was a solid eight-hour-a-night sleeper. As long as someone wasn't lying next to me waking me up. I was fortunate to have a serious relationship with a man years after my cruise, who also liked having his own room. When we moved in together, we both had what we wanted: emotional, physical, mental and spiritual companionship. All of that, with great sex and our own bedrooms was delightful. I loved having my own room and highly recommend it!

That evening, I met my table mates who became like family. The manager, of the enormous restaurant we dined in, also made himself known to me. His fierce eye contact combined with his plea for me to be sure to let him know if I needed anything, set the stage for defining "anything." His presence and hospitality were fervent, as was his determination to spoil me.

The next morning, there he was again. Francesco was alert and focused on me. I was dining alone when he zipped over and offered to walk me, to what he considered, the best seat in the house. He was oozing with passion like a vibrant flower with a captivating scent - impossible to ignore. His attentive service and good looks were charming. My naive innocence didn't realize I was a target as a single woman on a cruise ship… alone. Duh! I was truly moving about my life with the purity of a child, in a woman's body, expanding my state of wonder and awareness. My life had been scripted for me, up until these years of choice, where my purity had a platform to express itself through wonder, and the woman in me had the opportunity to sample life and all of its flavors.

I needed to learn some things, that my mind would not have allowed, had I known what was coming in advance. I did enjoy the new wonder and curiosity in my life. It made me feel more wildly alive. From that place, I didn't have to know everything in advance. I lived more in the present moment were there was a natural flow and things just lined up. It was like living as nature herself. Which felt very different from letting other people's opinions control my life. It was time for me to learn what I needed and what I wanted. Exploration was the best way for me to learn what I liked and didn't like. The explorer in me had a gratitude for the mystery of life and wanted to delve into its expression within me. From that place, I felt spacious. Life was rich in flavor; a caveat to dream.

That first evening, despite the enormity of the elegant dining facility, Francesco found his way to me so quickly I didn't see him coming. He was like a quarterback eyeing his wide receiver. I could feel him spot me, even if I couldn't see where he was in the room. He sent a bottle of wine to me that first night that I shared with my table mates. The next morning, I received more of his affection and attention. My cappuccino was frothed and crossing the gorgeous dining hall headed toward me before I got to my seat. It was as if he knew the moment, I left my cabin. The foreplay had begun.

Naples

When I stepped off the ship to explore Naples later that morning, I had a dozen Francesco's coming at me from every direction. Pouring me coffee and compliments and offering me invitations to lunch, dinner and more. I felt like a movie star walking the red carpet. I had never heard or seen men in the states be as outwardly open about their thoughts and feelings about me. These men didn't hold back. It was amazing and overwhelming, at the same time. I was a little shy about it but it felt good. I had been to Italy before but never alone, and never with my heart opening in such a profound way. I could feel and sense the world's beauty, within and around me, in tangible ways.

After sampling the delicacies of Naples in the form of: foods, shopping, and sites, I returned to the ship with a big "grazie" in my heart and in my hands. The men showered me with attention that I was not used to. It was wonderful to hear them say so many sweet things out loud. I certainly didn't go around thinking those things about myself. It made me appreciate hearing the things they were thinking. It was far nicer than a whistle. My new habit of falling in love with myself and valuing me was outwardly realized by their comments. They truly put a smile on my face, even if it did make me blush. You might say I was being objectified, and I wouldn't deny that, but at this time in my life their attention was an important reflection that made me see more of my own beauty. I do have nice legs and a warm smile but didn't acknowledge them, at that time. I do now and I'm not trying to boast. I'm merely appreciating my body and these men who helped me to see more of my own beauty, through their eyes and unedited mouths.

I walked back to my cabin giggling to myself about how their words and sweet gifts made me feel good inside. The men of Naples gave many things to me; including a heart-shaped pizza that I was carrying back to my room. Thanks to a pizza shop owner, who whisked me off the street insisting I needed to try his pizza. I told him I was pressed for time. He was sure he could make me a pie and have it ready to go, in no time and at no charge. His kindness and generosity convinced me to wait. The smell coming from his old-fashioned, stone oven was intoxicating. I could not say no.

Once the pizza was done, he slid the wooden paddle under it, and into a box it went. He turned and presented it to me, on one knee. Like a proposal... making me giggle. It was a work of art with fresh basil on top of hot melting ricotta and mozzarella cheese, layered on top of his bright red, homemade sauce. The masterpiece was presented on a custom shaped dough in the form of a heart! That put a huge smile on my face as you can image. I reached in and ripped off a piece of the crust to sample it in front of him. It was delizios!

I was savoring the moments of my day as I rounded the corner of the ship, headed toward my cabin when I saw Francesco walking toward me. I had not seen him outside the restaurant and quickly convinced myself it wasn't him. My mind went toward figuring out where my key was as I approached my door. I jostled it out of my bag without dropping my pizza and flowers and slid it in the door. That's when I felt his heavy breathing on the back of my neck, which sent delightful shivers up my spine. He was like a wild animal hunting me. I turned to look up at him as the door clicked open. He pushed his body up against mine and together we tumbled into my room. His jet-black hair, fell against my forehead when I spun around to face him. His dark eyes possessed me. He smelled and felt good up close. I smiled and nodded for more.

His hands ran up the sides of my body. I bent sideways to drop the pizza box on the floor, along with the flowers I had been given. He pulled me back up and like two flamingo dancers, our bodies were glued together as one. He led the dance by stepping toward me, forcing me to step back. Until I was pinned against the wall. His eyes and breath feasted on my feminine form with a hunger that made me weak and willing to submit. His primal nature unleashed reminded me of animals in the wild. Wolves came to mind. When a male wolf chooses a female, she's the one who decides and invites him in but, it's his hunger for her that chemically and energetically calls her forth. She drops her defenses and submits to him. I knew that feeling from a Taste of Brazil. He had that same ferocious longing for me and it was intoxicating. It drew me toward him and made me want to be devoured. I was more in touch with my own body with men who were connected to their hearts. Their active emotional bodies projected a magnetism I could not reject.

Francesco ravished my skin with his red lips and soft tongue. The intensity of his passion, in the way he held my body, while generously kissing me, made me hot and wet. He wasn't in his mind he was his body and that turned me on. I wanted him as much as he wanted me, by the way that he kissed me. He worked his way down my neck biting, licking, and kissing me. Oh my god, all of those different sensations awakened my body. I wanted him to have me as much he wanted me. He unbuttoned my blouse and held my breasts in his hands like peaches. He smiled and complimented them before attacking my nipples with his pleasurable techniques, that told my body that he loved every square inch of me.

My body felt like it was the fruit of life and that he needed it for his own survival. I was still new to the varieties of pleasure my body could enjoy and it wasn't until a new touch, technique or area of my body was explored, did I realize that pleasure for myself. Francesco quickly took me to new heights by his attention to detail, in the way he explored every area of my body. As if I were a sample platter from the neck down. The time he took to cover every square inch of my skin, on the way down to his knees was a delightful full body high for me.

My excitement intensified when he got to my waist and slid his hands up under my skirt, while kissing my stomach and nibbling on the sides of my hips. Wow, that felt so good. I had never had my hips sucked and nibbled on like that before. I loved every suspenseful moment but began to feel shy about him going down on me. That was a learned habit through shame. That temporal thought vanished by the way he whipped off my panties, in one forceful tug. He buried his head between my thighs and devoured me. The combination of standing and being taken in this way made me feel naughty and turned on. My legs locked into a firm position, giving me a sense of control and an ability to thrust forward, as he parted my lips to secure his position on my clitoris.

This man knew what he was doing. His steady rhythm was a one-way-ticket to paradise for me. Oral sex wasn't something I was comfortable receiving but Francesco, and some of the men who had come before him, helped me to discover that oral is a pleasure that - no woman should live without. Having not been prepared, somehow allowed me to receive and accept the pleasure that was being thrust between my thighs. My habitual mind could not get in the way, which allowed Francesco to take me all the way home... to paradise. That also had a lot to do with his enjoyment. A man who likes to give oral, is a hero to me. I grabbed the back of his head as I trembled and moaned in complete delight.

He pulled his head out from underneath my skirt and got up off of his knees. I pulled him close to me and whispered a sweet thank you in his ear. I was still feeling the pulsating ecstasy in my body, when I let him know he needed a condom to have sex with me, assuming that was where he was headed next. I was wrong. He had time constraints and had to go. He said he would be prepared for more, next time. Then he pushed his broad chest against my breasts. His crisp, white, button-down shirt had the faint smell of a cologne that was more like an aphrodisiac. I don't typically like most colognes but it was so faint and so masculine it was just the right amount. That waft sealed our moment in my senses, like a marker in time. He gave me a hug and said sweet things about what he had just enjoyed. Those words made me hot for him again. He kissed my forehead, before sweeping out the door, like a gust of wind. In a flash... he was gone.

'Oh, my goodness! Did that just happen?' so I thought to myself. The ship's horn sounded, meaning we were pushing off, but in its own way answering my question. "Yes, that did just happen!" I scratched my head, giggled, pulled up my panties, tossed my foxy locks, and smiled to myself thinking, 'I couldn't have dreamed that up.' That wasn't even something I imagined but now it was a living memory and fantasy come to life. My body was happy, satisfied, grateful, and eager to dig into my pie. You know what I mean. The delicious, custom-made pizza that witnessed my fantasy come to life. It was patiently waiting for me. As I picked it up, I said to it, "That will be our little secret." Which was the case, until now. (I can't believe I'm sharing this with all of you!) I felt the ship tug toward the sea. I climbed onto my bed and pulled the pizza box onto my lap, and ate my heart out.

Sicily

When we pulled up to Sicily the next day, I fell in love. The quaint charm of its hilltop town, cobblestone streets, and various ruins throughout captivated me. I was excited to dive into one of its many shops but their laid-back culture was more about lifestyle, than making money. The store owners were all closing their shops for lunch just as our entire ship arrived. I was shocked and educated, all at the same time. What a concept and a great perspective! I got to see my own narrow-minded myth of the American work ethic and its boasted moral benefit. These Italians cherished relaxation and lifestyle. How about that?! American's weren't afraid to work and neither were these people, but they weren't afraid to enjoy life and I found that fascinating.

Our unconscious enslavement in the U.S. didn't leave room for people to consider a laid-back lifestyle. That' been made impossible. Most would agree that each year it's more difficult to keep up the same standard of living. The Italians didn't stand in the back of their shop and scarf down food in between customers. They took long lunches and enjoyed socializing with friends and family. American's have learned to pride themselves on over-working. The Italians took on an unapologetic attitude about their way of life. I loved how these kinds of new perspectives shifted my own perceptions about life.

Since an entire town of shops shut down within minutes of us arriving, I followed suit and went to a cafe to enjoy the tastes of Sicily. I ran into a soccer team on my way. That was the extent of my sexual encounters in Sicily. Yep, a whole team of men who showered me with gorgeous smiles, hello's and hugs. They pointed me in the direction of a café with the best cannoli's in town. They were right. They were mind-blowingly good. After a walk through the city, the shops opened back up and I was able to purchase some gorgeous lingerie. Sicily was rich in color, attitude and flavor. I purchased a few beautiful scarves that captured the style and vibrancy of the island before I made my way back to the ship. The tippy-toe of Italy's boot was a kick-off, for more decadent and unexpected things to come.

Back at Sea

Francesco beamed when he saw me at the formal dinner that evening. He had a way of moving with a swiftness and grace, across the Olympic sized dining room, toward me. Then he'd hypnotize me by circling our table, making discrete eye contact with me from every angle. Those dark eyes and mischievous smile zapped me with sexual hunger. He could undress me in public and make me blush. That evening, he dropped me a note as he placed my napkin on my lap. I excused myself from the table to use the ladies' room to read it. The magician masterfully found a way to walk past me before I entered and whispered, "You are the most beautiful woman in this room!" I giggled and, 'poof!' he was gone.

His note was romantic and sweet. I appreciated how he expressed himself poetically. He also explained that he was risking his job by coming to my side of the ship but couldn't resist my beauty. It was sweet of him to say such things to me but I had no expectations of seeing him again or jeopardizing his job. Even if I did appreciate his words and oral skills. My evening was already planned. I was joining my table mates to attend a show after dinner. I smiled to myself in appreciation for his alluring invite but had no desire to meet up with him. I returned to my table and enjoyed an amazing meal with some wonderful company and headed to the lounge with my table-mates afterwards.

My new friends were two married couples; one from Italy and the other from Japan. The five of us had grown close because of our seating at our main table, and the great laughter we enjoyed

253

together. The Italians loved to drink and insisted on drinks before and after the show. I don't drink alcohol often. When I do, one is enough for me but the peer pressure was intense and the drinks kept coming. The last one put me over. I knew I had to get to my room, and fast, because I was done. I excused myself and made it to the elevator wishing I had bread crumbs to follow to find my cabin. The ship was now a large puzzle that I needed to piece together to find my way home.

Needless to say, I got lost and turned around a couple of times before landing on a bench on the outside deck. Lured by the sounds of the ocean and quite frankly… being lost. It was cold but I figured I could sit for a minute and find my way back to my room. That minute may have been twenty because I was startled awake when I heard Francesco's deep voice ordering the crew, "Pronto!" That woke me up. I had passed out on the bench. It wasn't clear what he was commanding of them but I knew his voice and was grateful to know I had help. He knew where my cabin was and could direct me back.

I reached my hand up like a flag and he saw it. He said something in Italian as he swooped down to rescue me. His sweet words were full of heart. I didn't need to know his language to know what they mean. I felt them. I asked him if he could take me to my room. His tone got serious as he spoke to his employees and sent them on their way. Then he helped me up. I slid my arm around his waist and pulled him close; wanting the warmth and the support of his body next to mine. It felt good to have his support. Our walk to my cabin seemed long. It gave me time to come back to life as the cool evening wind and cat nap sobered me up. As did his kisses when the door closed behind us. I felt weightless the way he whisked me up onto my bed, landing between the two towel swans.

Francesco poured me a glass of water and sat next to me. I gulped it down. He looked like he was going to say goodbye. Then he asked if I needed help putting on my pj's or if I just wanted to climb under the covers. He pulled my hair back and just stared into my eyes, petting my face with the back of his hand. Telling me my skin was beautiful and asking if there was anything else, I needed before he left. Each of those gestures made me want him inside of me. There's something about genuine compassion and care from a man that turns me on.

He was now my hero having saved me from the cold and gotten me back to my room. Of course, I wanted to reward him. I couldn't resist his dark eyes and his caring nature. I pulled his collar toward my face and smelled the grappa still lingering on my lips. I gave him a black licorice kiss. He sucked and bit my lips tenderly while telling me how much he loved the softness of them. Between his compliments and passionate kisses there was no way I was going to let him leave. I started to unbutton his crisp white tuxedo shirt. He graciously thanked me for the invitation to stay longer before saying more.

He confessed, "Bella, I don't have much time now. I waited for you two hours ago when I did have the time."

I told him I was sorry but had not agreed to his invite and never had the opportunity to communicate it to him before I left the dining room. Once I left, I forgot. I apologized for that too. He said he understood and then took my hand and kissed it.

From his lips, my hand went behind his head. I pulled him toward me and said, "I bet you have enough time right now."

That was my consent, to what was going to be no foreplay sex. The foreplay, for me, had actually begun in his 'act of service' when he rescued me. Everything that he did after that made me want him more. His soft touch of my skin, getting me water, and not assuming any of that meant that he could jump my bones was its own invitation.

His body didn't hide the excitement of my "let's do this" consent. I could see it and feel it when he pushed his body up against mine. The only thing between me and him was my formal dress. A dress that made me feel like a queen, who was now back in her castle, needing assistance in its removal. The sound of the zipper running down my back was a freedom that made my whole-body smile. The air against my skin was tingly. I looked up at him and loved what I saw. His shirt was fully unbuttoned. There's something sexy about clothes half-on that turns me on. His tan skin and broad chest were framed by his wide-open tuxedo shirt. The scene was as sexy as you can imagine. He leaned over and kissed me and worked down my neck as he unzipped his pants. They fell to the floor and I believe I said, "Wow!" out loud. He returned his attention to my body to finish kissing me all the way down the front and landing right where he left off last. I loved how he indulged in my body, like it was a wellspring of energy that fed him. I was wet and ready for him to enter me, and that was all that I wanted when he pulled his head up and looked deeply into my eyes.

He pulled away from me for a moment and out came a condom. He lifted it into the air and said, "As you requested Madam!"

I giggled and thanked him. His strong body mounted mine and ever so slowly he made his way inside of my sacred center. This man was expressive and made his appreciation known by verbalizing the pleasure he was experiencing upon entering my body. I could feel his feelings and my own through his emotional expression. His words and sounds deepened our intimacy. We both had a lot to express when we opened our hearts and bodies to one another.

Francesco's eyes got wide and his moan got loud when he made it completely inside of me. He stopped, looked into my eyes, and spoke Italian. I didn't need to know the language; I could sense the meaning in his words by the feeling in his body. The sweat that dripped off the tip of his forehead and landed on my lips was a salty treat I licked and savored as the depth and intensity of his body expanded within me.

Our lips and breath were one. Our lovemaking was slow, deep and passionate. I could sense his spirit and feel his heart. Our bodies were gripped in a magnetism that produced its own heat. I felt the tug of the ocean beneath us as our bodies alchemized in a fire I could feel on my skin and inside my sacred center. We rode the waves of ecstasy until his final, slow and riveting thrust became an inferno of pulsating energy I could feel throughout my body. His loud moan scorched the air and his large, muscular body went limp. It was breathtaking to feel the combustion of our bodies and to witness his explosion.

I shimmed myself from beneath him, to get some air. He came back to life a minute later. His eyes were sparkly and alert. He seemed more present and blissful than ever. He was mumbling, "Oh Bella, Oh Bella." He headed to the bathroom, washed up, and came out with a glowing smile on his face. We locked eyes with one another as he buttoned his shirt, savoring every moment we had left together. He was fully present with me and didn't say a word. He just breathed, smiled, and stared into my eyes. Then he bent down to kiss me.

He whispered in a warm, sweet tone. "Bella, you are unlike any woman in what you do to me. I will never forget this feeling with you."

Those words touched my heart and I didn't forget them. When I woke the next morning with a throbbing head from the alcohol, and a sore 'you know what,' I could not deny what I had done the night before. Unbelievable. I sat up in my hangover state dying of thirst. Flung back the sheets and got out of bed. My pillow followed and hit the floor, along with Francesco's name tag that bounced and hit my toes. There was the evidence, right in my face. The man I believed I would not be meeting up with again, came to my rescue, and escorted me home. It was mysterious in the way that not being attached to: people, places or things freed me of expectations. And, constantly brought me unexpected surprises as life became its own adventure.

Alexandria Egypt

I laid low that morning and was reminded of why I don't drink. I made my way to the spa and took a steam, and then a yoga class to churn out the toxins. I lounged and nurtured myself all day; staring at the sea, reading and rehydrating. Practicing self-care is such an important part of living. That if you walk away with nothing from this book but becoming aware of your own self-care regimen - then I will have succeeded in teaching you something vitally important. My day at sea, ended with me skipping diner that evening and going to bed early. The hermit in me appreciated my day alone.

The next morning, I felt refreshed as we docked at the port of Alexandria, Egypt. The mystical land of Egypt had made a lasting impression on me two years earlier. I was returning with new eyes to see and ears to hear… more. I got off the ship and immediately onto one of the buses that were touring the city and Alexandria library. The bus was already packed full when I stepped on but the tour director, a young handsome Egyptian man, waved me over to sit next to him. He jumped up and pointed to the window seat and quickly moved his papers and name tags to make room for me. Egypt had a very special way of making room for (all of) me.

The tour was amazing. My favorite stop was the library where everything felt alive. It was intense. It brought me back to that multi-dimensional realm that Egypt opens within me. The artifacts held ancient secrets, memories, and energy that put me in a trance. It felt like the top of my head had opened up and expanded. I could not hear our guide anymore but I could feel everything, as if worlds beyond time and space were communicating a knowledge to me. Information that wasn't to be read but rather remembered. Some might call that experience a download; in the way information comes in volumes and you feel altered by it. Our tour guide was very observant and noticed something was happening to me. He kept a gentle and interested eye on me. We had an age difference of about ten years. He may have thought it was half that, when he invited me for a private tour of his town when our group tour ended. I accepted his invitation when we got off of the bus.

Another unexpected adventure awaited me. Anubis possessed an innocent sweetness, while projecting a mature and scholarly demeanor. He opened my eyes to a part of Egypt I had never seen, by taking me into the town where tourists don't go. Like a young kid, I pointed at things I had never seen before like entire carcass' hanging outside delis and restaurants. People milled about the streets, shopping with their families. Women covered their hair and bodies in black as a part of their religious tradition. The whole scene felt like I was back in time. In order to respect their tradition and to blend in more, Anubis stopped and bought me a scarf, to cover my bare arms and cleavage, before taking me to a popular local restaurant to eat. I observed the cultural differences and their emphasis on 'family and religion are everything.' It was clear I was an outsider in this culture by the way I was dressed but I still enjoyed their traditional foods, unique music, dusty deserts streets, and packed restaurant full of families speaking in their native tongue.

My senses were stimulated by the rawness of their culture. Years later, I would experience a similar "back in time" culture in Morocco where women are deemed disposable, with patriarchal control of the people, despite the modern-day marriage of their king to an empowered woman with an engineering degree. She had apparently since my visit had "gone into hiding." We know what that could mean. I digress.

Back to my tour guide, soon to be new lover. When we finished eating lunch, he asked if I wanted to drive up the coast before returning me to the ship. I agreed. It turned out that he lived along the coast and had just moved into a new place and wanted to show it to me. He lived on the top floor of a high rise that looked over the Mediterranean Sea. Which I caught a better view of when we stepped off the elevator and into his large apartment. The glistening ocean seemed to leap right into his living room. Inside of his home he still appeared shy and was polite, so I did not see it coming when he asked for permission to kiss me. I affectionally giggled and said, "Yes." His soft, dark eyes looked deeply into mine.

His hand reached up and pushed my hair off my cheek. He said, "You are a beautiful and kind woman who has made my day more special." Those sweet words made me feel appreciated and honored. His kindness and compassion would lead to me being a source of inspiration to him. In ways that could only be reached through a spark of sexual freedom he had not known. But none of that was something I saw coming.

He kissed me ever so softly as if not to hurt me. He reached down and took my hand and led me further into his apartment. The tour ended in his bedroom where our clothes came off and his condom went on. I did not foresee that, even ten minutes before it happened. For some reason, the spontaneity of it all gave me little time to enforce old thinking. It allowed me to go with the flow, and each time healing happened. Not in ways my mind could even understand. It was more enjoyable to live in the moment, even if my mind was ill prepared.

Anubis had very little experience in the intimacy department. Although, I wasn't wet and ready, he was gentle. There wasn't blazing chemistry but more of a curiosity and an openness that led me to accepting the unexpected sexual encounter. I do believe it was more for him than me. His culture had caged him in a life of restraint or bodily repression. I learned more about that after he quickly and quietly came. Women his age withheld sex until marriage. I was the first woman, and the second female, he had ever had sex with. He explained the dynamics of the majority of women his age being controlled by their culture and religious dogma. They were taught to withhold sex to ensure a marriage proposal. He was sincerely thankful to me for having sex with him. You might imagine how frustrating and lonely it could be for a young man in his mid to late 20's looking to explore his sexuality and having little to no opportunity.

Anubis knew he didn't want to marry yet and wasn't sure where he stood steeped in a Muslim culture that seemed as restricted as his Christian upbringing. He said he didn't have anyone to talk to about these things and was surprised how comfortable it was to share his feeling with me. He seemed to get a load off, more than just his mind, as he held me close. I noticed that once he ejaculated, he was far more open about his feelings. That is an interesting thing about men that I find fascinating, beautiful and special.

It was nice to see him temporarily freed from his shackles of societal control when he opened up. He was more philosophical and reflective when he landed in his authentic nature. There was a certainty in his stature as he spoke about his views on life. He matured before my eyes as he stepped into his Higher Self. I found it sexy in the way he dared to question life to honor his own instincts. I liked that about him and was glad that we had the intimate time together. It brought forth a whole other dimension and a depth of understanding from within him. Our intimacy was a gateway to more of his own unique power.

This particular sexual experience was about me giving to someone else. I knew what it was like to feel trapped and to be judged. I didn't burn my steak and overthink things. I allowed the experience to unfold and as a result I witnessed our intimacy as a healing salve for him. He got to be heard and to open up in ways that he would not have otherwise. I didn't plan or expect any of that but I did observe that my heart and my body touched his life in a positive way. From my own experience I know that when I verbalize my thoughts and feelings with close friends, I have an opportunity to see them outside of myself. Which helps me shift out of one way or pivot toward another way within my multidimensional self. The point is, I don't remain stuck by keeping it all in my head - I move deeper within.

It was a short sexual experience but a significant opening for Anubis to see things more clearly. Our time together came to an end when we both noticed the time. We needed to get dressed and get me to the ship right away. The final horn was blowing as he pulled up as close as he could to the steps, thanks to his tourism badge. He ejected the CD from his car stereo and handed it to me as I jumped out of his car.

He said, "Take this to remember me."

Our quality time spent together would-be reason enough to remember him but I took the CD and ran to the ship. The crew at the top of the steps took my hand as I made my final leap onboard. I waived back at Anubis and to Egypt with my heart full of gratitude for another unexpected experience; an adventure I could have never planned.

Cyprus

Back on the ship, I showered and snuggled under the covers and took a nap before going to dinner. Francesco had flowers sitting in front of my seat, indicating with his eyes and his head that they were for me. It was a spectacular arrangement of flowers with a lotus in the center of the arrangement. I couldn't take my eyes off of its exotic splendor. Next to the flowers, was a full glass of wine that I was not going to drink but I certainly appreciated him spoiling me. I had my fill of alcohol and was content with my self-care regimen, which required me upholding strong boundaries as everyone at my table was drinking. The growing hermit in me wanted more time alone in between the excursions on land. I did my disappearing act that night by slipping out of the restaurant after a bite of my dessert. My mind was on Jesus who I knew I'd be seeing the next day when we arrived in Cyprus. My Machu Picchu lover would be waiting for me when we docked on his island the next morning.

That evening, I journaled and reflected on my time at sea and all of the unexpected encounters that snuck up on me. The only man I thought I might be romantic with on my entire trip was the man I would be seeing next. Life was purposely blowing my mind and challenging me to uproot the old. The new had no context in the false narratives of the old. My heart and my body were a healing salve me and as it turned out, for others. I was learning to fall in love with my own body and to make peace with sex. The spiritual teachings I had consumed for the years during my transformation, seemed to bypass the importance of honoring and appreciating the body and being in touch with its information system. I possessed a deep love in my heart that I could share with others, once I shared it with myself.

Perhaps a modern-day interpretation of evolution hasn't been painted through the eyes of enough women for us to see more. My take includes sexuality because that was an area I needed to heal. It's interesting that sex has been portrayed in pornographic ways and then held in society as acceptable only in marriage and in long-term partnership. It was difficult for me to have these experiences because of what I had learned and believed. Control over our bodies through various systems of control is disturbing.

It was mind-blowing for me to extract lies tied to virginal ways having been deemed holy. Along with the idea that God was in the sky judging me. Religion taught me how to judge myself, not how to not love me. The tenderness of these men helped me to see my fears around my body and the judgements that were once held in place when I didn't face them. Each of these men, without knowing it, were helping me to feel safe in my own body. Their affection was giving me an opportunity to heal the relationship with my body.

My bravery of taking an honest look at myself resulted in me reframing my own beliefs through new experiences. Religion had taught me conditional love. My evolution led to me awakening from ignorance. I came to determine God wasn't a man but rather an embodiment of love, and it was my responsibility to love myself. Not for some image in the sky to love me. The love I was after was in my own heart and it could be felt through my body.

I filled my journal that night with my thoughts, feelings, and experiences. I dozed off with my pen in hand and woke the next morning ready to write my next chapter on the shores of Cyprus. I showered, put on my bathing suit, threw on a cute sundress and headed to the deck. Within seconds I spotted Jesus waving up at me. It felt good to see his smiling face at the port. I came down the steps to his wide-open arms, and giggled as he swept me up and into his heart. We kissed, smiled and stared into each other's eyes, before making our way to the mysterious destination he insisted I must see.

We drove along the spectacular coast, where I took in the gorgeous, green-blue waters. The warm air whipped my hair around as we chatted and held hands. He drove us to my enormous surprise which was Aphrodite's Rock. A tribute to the Goddess of Love herself. I had no idea when he nicknamed me in Peru that her legend was linked to his land. What a spectacular rock formation, as big as a house and surrounded by crystal clear waters, all in her honor.

He parked the car and we walked toward the rock. I was giggly with excitement. I love rocks and collect them all the time, but this one wouldn't be coming home with me. When we got to the base of it, he pulled me toward him and rested my back against the rock. The ocean seemed to dance all around us as we kissed. The long stares into each other's eyes, the big smiles on our faces, and the wet kisses we shared made me feel like no one else existed in the entire world, but us. Each new moment in my life was a page-turner. I could not have imagined what I was living or how good I could feel.

The wind against my skin, the ocean roaring with power, and the chemistry between us heightened the magnificence of creation. We both wanted to peel our clothes off right there and make love. That wasn't possible as we were at the foot of a tourist attraction, even if we were the first to arrive. He took my hand and we walked along the beach to a private area where we could not be seen. He brought a blanket and the two of us tumbled on top of it, the moment it hit the sand. We laughed and kissed like teenagers without a care in the world. He slipped off my bikini bottoms and undid his swim trunks. I felt his throbbing penis and held it tight, noticing my growing comfort with a man's body. There was a pleasure and an appreciation of the masculine form that I wanted to pay tribute to. Not for the sake of duty, but for my own selfish pleasure. I was genuinely curious and intrigued when I allowed my own inner affection to come outward.

We had an amazing bond. Our bodies returned to a depth of connection we had known under the full moon in Peru. Our hearts naturally opened to one another. His life was dedicated to living his highest and greatest potential and it showed in his eyes, in his touch, and in his presence. The sand, the sunshine, and the sea were all ours. When I moved out of my learned beliefs around my body, I felt life from the inside out.

The beauty of Cyprus made its mark on me through my connection with Jesus and the experience we shared that day. When he saw me off at the dock hours later, I felt grateful for our adventure; having been touched by the sea, the sun, the monumental rock, his lips, hands, eyes, and penis. He was conscious and present, gentle and loving; and full of fire like a warrior. I felt respected, appreciated and cherished by him. Two years and seven thousand miles apart did not erase our connection. Our love was an example of my learning to live without attachment. Without a need to possess or to be possessed. There was a freedom and a capacity for great love beyond man-made rules, restrictions, conditions, expectations and repression. I was feeling more wildly alive each day as I authored my own life.

Santorini & Marmaris

Our next destination was Santorini and although I was approached by several men there and at our next stop in Turkey, I was so taken by the terrain I could not focus on anything else. I walked the town of Santorini and enjoyed the beautiful white and blue landscape and many shops. When I arrived in Marmaris I did a private excursion with about thirty other people, on a small boat that changed my life. We took in the most

breathtaking rock formations and pristine waters along a cove. I watched two wild dolphins jump from the water inviting me to come play. You can consider the dolphins as my lovers in Marmaris because my heart leapt out of my chest when they came out of the water and into my life. I begged the Captain to stop the boat so that we could get in the water right there and then. I had never seen water like that in my life. There was something magnetic about it.

Thankfully, the Captain kindly stopped the boat and let us all get in right there where the dolphins had jumped next to our boat. When I got into that heavenly oasis of water, I swam over to the unique rock formations that jetted out like a castle, making a majestic cove that took me inward. I felt like I had entered a gateway to a land before time. That's the best way I can describe the feeling of being transported. It was like LSD but not drug induced.

I held onto the side of the towering rock and went into an altered state. My consciousness expanded and the top of my head opened up and time collapsed. My body was in the water, I could faintly hear the people around me as my multidimensional self was tangible in my body. I expanded into a bliss-like state of spaciousness where more knowledge lied within me. My heart seemed to lift up and out of my chest expanding in all directions. I felt like an orbiting universe. This may sound outrageous to you but something deep and profound happened to me in that cove. If rocks and water could speak, they would have told me they held codes and ancient information, and in fact they did communicate that to me.

In my altered state, I allowed my curiosity to ask questions inwardly. I began to telepathically communicate with the presence of that information as it answered back. My multidimensional self knew this was the clearest and most natural state of communication. That we as humans are the advanced technology but we had access it within us. Like someone taking my call, I quickly received answers. When I asked about the water and why it felt mind expansive and memory encoded, I received a confirmation that it was both, and that that technology was also inside of me. When I asked how it was possible, the answer came to my mind that, 'Thousands of years ago, a highly developed race of human life used the water and the rocks to store libraries of information.' The answer made sense to my heart, even though my mind wanted to doubt. There was so much more available for us to know and to become but we would need to evolve and let go of limitation. Those particular waters were an activation and I felt it in every cell of my body. I never spoke about my experience with anyone but now that I am coming of the closet as a multidimensional being who believes in my limitless nature - I have nothing to hide.

Choosing to become my highest and greatest potential wasn't forced on me. It was my choice and that choice seemed to continually bring me unimaginable experiences that brought new realizations. Life would continually reveal to me - the limitlessness of creation. The more I experienced and learned, the more I realized how little I knew.

I had never even heard of Marmaris, Turkey until I was aboard that cruise ship, where I found myself dipping into the magical waters of the Aegean Sea. The two dolphins were the stealthy culprits that led me into the depths. When I returned to the small boat and got on deck, the breeze hitting my skin gave me chills. That's just what I needed to ground back into my body. As we motored back to the ship, I stood like a bronze statue on deck. My eyes staring forward but my mind still expanding. I had acute sensations of clarity and precision that formed a marker in time, and gave me a 360-degree view of life. It was like seeing in all direction without moving my head. Whatever happened to me, call it a download, an activation or an altered state of consciousness; it changed me and I knew it. More of my spirit was embodied as my high-performance vehicle, and I felt the power of that engine in me. I left that port with more twinkle in my heart that can be seen in my eyes. Remembrance of who you are from the inside out, will do that to you.

Disembark

Before we returned to Genoa, Italy to disembark and say goodbye to the Mediterranean, I packed my grateful heart, my souvenirs of my hand-made leather shoes from Turkey, a white dress from Greece, scarves from Egypt, lingerie from Sicily and Francesco's name tag, that he told me I could keep. I hugged my table mates that morning and kissed them goodbye. Francesco found a quick window to swoop over and hug me, while whispering passionate words in both English and Italian in my ear. Our secrets would remain between us... until now.

I was onto a whole new adventure, and needed to turn my attention to navigating my own way, on land. I was headed to

Damanhur; an eco-village and spiritual community based at the foothills of the Alps in Chiusella Valley, Italy. The seed of Damanhur was planted in my mind after visiting my friend Joseph, who I had met on a trip to Israel years prior. When I visited him in California a year after we met, he received a picture book about the underground temples in Damanhur, the day I came to visit him. When we looked through his new book together, we were both fascinated with the underground temples. The people of Damanhur had chiseled them into existence. Me and Joseph both agreed we would one day visit Damanhur. This was my day.

Damanhur, was named after an Egyptian city and its main temple was dedicated to Horus. I connected with Horus in Egypt years earlier. The Temple of Humankind in Damanhur was my next destination, which was a 4–5-hour bus ride north. Off I went.

Chapter 28
Spider-Man

I certainly didn't suspect that sex was waiting for me in a spiritual community. But then again, I didn't think it was waiting for me in the Andes, or along the Mediterranean either. My mind was focused on seeing the underground temples. As usual, when I went into things with preconceived notions, the unexpected was waiting to seduce me. And that's exactly what happened when I entered the temple. I almost missed the grand entrance because I was too busy assuming it would be "grand." They did a great job hiding the mystery that lied beneath the ordinary community center entrance. My guide enjoyed watching my reaction when the elevator doors opened to the Temple of Humankind. The cool breeze and dark cave that appeared before my eyes was disorienting to me, because I wasn't expecting the generic elevator to be taking me an underground stone entryway.

To engage my instincts, my guide encouraged me to enter the room off of the elevator, to find the secret passageway that opened to the temple. There was no obvious door anywhere but I tuned in and walked over to the opposite right-hand side wall. I put my hand against the stone and pushed hard. Wallah! It opened to the mysteries within.

She smiled and said, "Good job!"

I was in. It was cold and dark but there was lighting, like you'd see inside of an old church. She turned on more lighting for me to see all of the art work that had been painted throughout the temple. There were also orbs and crystals placed throughout. The first thing I noticed was how I felt. The temples were constructed above a vortex of energy that gave me the sense of being spun in a circle. I had the same feeling in the some of the temples and pyramids in Egypt. It's that feeling you get from riding a rollercoaster.

It's important to remember we are made of energy and to become acquainted with that energy in our body. When life becomes about frequency and not financial wealth, you'll realize that your vibe determines everything. For me, when I began my transformation, I ended up on an energy healers table, I refer to him as Dr. Frankenstein in my first book (as a joke). He informed me that most of my energy centers were spinning the wrong direction, or that they were barely rotating. The psychologist I worked with before meeting him could read auras and taught me how to see them myself. I also took two reiki classes and got certified at his center to learn more about my energy.

Back to the temple. There was much to see on the stone walls. The artists of their community had painted the history of humanity in each room and along the corridors. It was like a time capsule about the human race. From the time of wild buffalos and Indians to modern-day genetically modified foods. I would guess by now they have added: the corona virus, masks, house arrest, distancing (which is not social), riots, protests, fires, voter fraud, vaccines, and the takedown of the globalists by the awakened global citizens of earth, to the walls in keeping our history up-to-date.

Upon completion of my solo tour, I was introduced to one of the male members of the community who invited me to dinner. Each of the members had a human name and an animal or insect name. Thankfully, I had no fear of spiders since Spider was my date for dinner. He enlightenment me about their Federation, including their take on marriage which was renewable each year. What a great concept! That seemed like a fair way for partners to check-in with each other every year. They could reflect on their year together and decide to renew or not. He said, it was uncommon for people to end their marriages after one, two or even three years but the option was there for them. Don't you think that's cool? I do.

With the speed of our learning at this phase of our evolutionary design I believe a renewable marriage makes sense. We are learning and growing rapidly. Consider the influence this marriage agreement would have on stomping out stagnation, that typically occurs in lengthy relationships. By checking-in each year both sides get to be honest with themselves. It seems it would keep relationships close, intentional, conscious, and accountable.

Some people may need to go through more relationships in this lifetime, depending on what they are here to learn. Look how I had to gather my lessons and knowledge outside of the traditional set-up. There was much for me to learn about my body and myself through the diversity I experienced. None of which could have been learned in the confinements of repression. The final positive I see about their marriage renewal is that it removes obligatory shame. There's less room for guilt when there's acceptance for the completion of a relationship.

Which I believe is healthier than forcing people to stay in a limited growth and unhappy situations.

Their group was called The Federation, and they chose to live by their own rules and constructs that nurtured their individual spirits and their need for togetherness. Their consensual system was designed around their values, needs, and wants. Although the temples made their community unique, they were hidden below the ground. The town itself was more of a European village of people who lived in houses or flats. What made their village different was their intentional community constructs. They voted on rules and regulations that they upheld together. This gave them a sense of freedom and togetherness. I got a taste of that combo when Spider-Man walked me to my charming hotel that evening after our dinner together.

Spider-Man was a dark-haired, handsome, Italian man about 5'10" and I would guess about 35 years old. He was more introverted so I didn't sense any sexual advances when he walked me to my room. He was polite and considerate. I accepted his offer to retrieve my bags from the main community center, where I had left them earlier that day when I arrived. I was dying to shower and brush my teeth, and did both in the time that it took him to get back. I slipped back into my dress when I heard him knock and was happy to see my gargantuan bags at his sides. I was ready to get into my pj's as it had been a long day. I thanked him for dinner and his help. I asked if I could give him a hug. He politely nodded yes and smiled. I threw my arms and semi-wet body around him. That's when I felt a surge of sexual energy from him that ignited my own. It was like a switch being turned on. What I thought was a goodnight hug, turned out to be a torch of sexual arousal. I was taken by surprise by what seemed to spark in the middle of my room.

When he finally did let me go, I looked up at him and smiled. I was now turned on. He calmly asked if he could bring me pleasure before he left? I giggled out loud and thought to myself, 'Hmmm? What does that mean?' I said nothing but gave an inquisitive look.

That's when he said, "Let me show you."

My adorable, dimly lit room, cast an eerie shadow on the oxblood, velvet chaise lounge behind him. Like a spider he made a quick move and spun me around and asked me to sit down on the chase. I felt like a fairy the way he swept me up and around. He told me to lay back and make myself comfortable. He knelt on the floor and looked up at me, asking if he could touch my legs. I nodded yes, and watched his long fingers slowly graze the surface of my skin. He had an incredibly healing touch that made me take long, slow, deep breaths, relaxing more into my body. I was suddenly under his spell.

He continued to ask permission which I found delightful. It made me feel respected. I then realized I had not put on any panties after I showered. Too late, his fingers were on their way up under my dress. Now he knew I was panty-less too. I needed to breathe again, to get out of my head because I was feeling nervous and excited at the same time. Taking a deep breath helped me to let go and to become more receptive. The act of receiving is a very different than the act of giving. There's a loss of control that requires a new level of openness.

That's when he looked up at me and said, "May I?"

His head at that moment was right between my thighs. There was something about his asking for permission that turned me on. I liked it a lot. And while everything in me screamed, "Yes, you may!" I still had to face my oral sex fears that had been elaborately assembled through shaming that area of my body, before I had a chance to better know it myself. Even though I was an adult and had just experienced oral sex a couple of days prior, those old programs were still running inside of me. I had to face them in order to change them. This was an amazing opportunity to enjoy pleasure, but my body and mind had old memories that got stirred up. It would have been easier for me to say no to him because my fear was strong, and it was trying to convince me to stop. I succeeded in receiving oral from Francesco so a part of me knew I could do this but I was still nervous and self-conscious. Spider-Man was my next test and opportunity to break free. Could I receive? Would my mind win over my body? As I wrestled with my mental torment, he patiently waited for my consent.

I took a deep breath and softly said, "Yes."

Spider-Man's face disappeared and I closed my eyes. I leaned my head back against the side of the chase, and fell into my breath. Which led me back into my body where I could feel myself "down there." I could not help but wonder if Spider-Man was in an open relationship, where intercourse outside of his relationship wasn't permitted but cunnilingus was? He didn't even kiss me. It was strange but I understood the complexities of open relationships were unique. The woman I met in Arizona who was committed to two men, told me she had very specific requests or rules for the men she lived with. When they dated other women, she was firm about: the time she wanted them home, and wearing condoms if they had sex. My other thought was, 'Is this a European thing?' What woman couldn't get used to all the cunnilingus? The clitoris being designed exclusively for pleasure - I was gaining an understanding of what that actual meant. And, how certain men had a gift for giving pleasure to that area.

Both Spider-Man and Francesco enjoyed giving oral and it showed. That's when I learned that their enjoyment was important to my own. Spider-Man was definitely in a league of his own when it came to oral. It seemed like seconds, in how quickly he took me out of my nervousness, and into my throbbing clitoris. By the way he attacked it with precision. Spiders paralyze their prey first, and that's exactly what it felt like he did to me. He firmly held my hips in place with one hand, and with the other he pushed back my pubic mound to expose my clitoris. Like placing me in his web and then devouring the juiciest part of me. It's worth mentioning that men need to remember that as a clitoris can be so tiny that by exposing it just enough you've upped the game. I didn't even know I could orgasm that quickly. It was a combination of exposing the area and then the tempo and pressure. He hit it out of the park!

When Spiderman left my room, I didn't even see him go because the unbelievable pleasure he ignited in my body, almost blinded me as a golden light blazed behind my closed eyes. Could the spirit of what people call God be felt and experienced in our body as an orgasm? Was guilt, shame, and a disconnect from my own body the things holding me back from experiencing that depth of light within me, and as me?

Well, it took shedding a lot of shame to get to the point of receiving pleasure. It was worth facing my fears to end up there. I was healing my past and clearing the way for what felt like heaven in my body. That didn't mean I needed to have sex all of the time, even though sex has become more important to me. It was about feeling my body and being connected to it in ways I had not been before.

Learning to have an orgasm was important. It was another level of surrender. It wasn't about doing nothing; it was more about allowing something more. The letting go of control of where my mind could take me, allowed my body to take me someplace even more beautiful. I'm more curious than ever about orgasms. I had never seen sex as a spiritual experience until I found myself outside of my marriage, and only after I gained a more intimate relationship with my own body. Thanks to Spiderman, I got the opportunity to; transform fear into light, pain into pleasure, and contraction into expansion.

Chapter 29
The Professor

The next day, I headed to Milan to spend the night. I mentioned earlier about the spiritual book that lifted my frequency and deepened my quest, "The Autobiography of a Yogi." Well, the author who goes by Yogananda created a worldwide organization called Self Realization Fellowship. I wanted to attend the Sunday lecture at his center in Milan the following morning, before I made my way to Switzerland. I had visited his centers in other parts of the world but this was the first one in Italy. I enjoyed the depth I felt in any one of his SRF halls, temples, or centers so the language barrier was irrelevant to me. After the service I took my elevated state to the train station in Milan. Where I boarded my silver vessel headed to Switzerland to visit a girlfriend from California, who had been promoted and transferred to Basel, Switzerland.

The next man to enter my life was on that train. He was scholarly and not someone who would flirt with a younger woman. My innocent charm and curiosity brought him out of his shell. I had no idea that our connection would follow me to Basel and eventually lead me to his house, a couple of doors down from my girlfriend's place. What are the chances? My learning curve of a lifetime was squeezed into this trip abroad, as I came to sample a variety of men from all walks of life. To better know the depth of my own character and to fall more deeply in love with the flesh of who I am.

My openness and genuine appreciation for people prompted one-on-one conversations that came easy, the more I learned who I was not. The sexual component of it all was a shocker to me but a vital step in helping me break out of the box of feminine and body shame. I do have a European or Mediterranean look to me, and roots that connect me to Italy, Romania, Germany, France and Wales. Perhaps my look, combined with these regions spun together the perfect setting for my growth?

I loved the regal feel of Switzerland and the smell of roasted chestnuts sold in paper bags on street corners. That I enjoyed eating while roaming the cobblestone streets. The diverse and interesting men I was encountering on my trip, were as unique and varied as the architectural styles represented throughout Switzerland. The newest style of man came in the form of a professor, who apparently was not to remain a man in passing. He had said goodbye to me after a long and intriguing conversation on the train, but we would come together again soon enough.

It was our intellectual chemistry that sparked our conversation. The scientist in me was intrigued. As I felt more comfortable in my own skin I accepted more of my natural intelligence. I did find the professor handsome but his brain is what attracted me, and the role that I played - as the assertive one. It felt comfortable and I liked that comfort. We were both delighted, as fate would have it, to be seeing each other again the following day. There was an unexpected window that opened up for me to go and see him. My girlfriend had a business meeting and I had two hours to fill. My instincts said, 'Go see The Professor!' I didn't overthink it. I acted on it. I walked right over to his house and knocked on his large, oak front door. I was traveling without a phone, relying on computer access to check emails. I never asked for his contact information, assuming I would not see him again. When we both walked the same direction after getting off of the train, I was able to see how close he lived.

His face lit up when he saw me. That made me feel good. He warmly invited me in, confessing he was in his study catching up on his work. He offered me a cup of tea and put on a fresh pot of water. His lovely historic stone home felt cozy. I asked if I could see his study when our tea was ready. I love books and figured he had lots. We walked through a stone corridor with our piping hot mugs as I took in his collection of unique artifacts from around the world. Things were beautifully displayed throughout his home. I felt like I was in a museum.

When we got to his study I didn't want to leave. The Professor was a brilliant scientist with more books on his shelves than I could count. He could engage in conversation for hours he had so much knowledge in his head. His mind made me wet and my body wanted to show him exactly how I felt. He had a sexual innocence about him that intrigued the alpha female in me. It was clear that he spent most of his time behind his large, hand-carved, mahogany desk. I observed his many degrees and awards across his enormous, built-in shelving unit. I noticed the picture of his deceased wife amongst his many keepsakes. He had lost his wife to cancer ten years prior and had no interest in remarrying. It was mostly due in part to his second love; seeking and sharing knowledge about science. Which kept him busy.

283

He didn't seek romance but his body was receptive to my advances and requests when I leaned against him and asked if I could kiss him. I surprised myself in how comfortable I felt in making advances. The delight in his eyes was emotional. This was new territory for me in making the first move but I felt an assurance that lived inside of me. This part of me didn't care if he rejected me or not. I knew what I wanted and I was going for it. I also noticed how much I liked the consent Spiderman sought and was happy to extend that same respect to someone else. The professor agreed to my request and pulled me closer. I could feel his nervous hand against my back and the tension in his body. He was vulnerable. I reached for his hand and asked him to follow me. I led him to the chair behind his desk and asked him to sit down.

He could tell I was the one in charge and a part of him liked it, and so did I. He smiled at me as he sat down making it easier for me to look into his eyes. My instinct was to climb onto his lap like a kitty cat, so I did. This time I kissed him, deeper and longer. It was clear that it had been a while since he was romanced by the way he held his breath. However, from the waist down he was enjoying himself as I felt him rise to the occasion when we kissed. Things were alive and well below the belt.

A scholarly man, professionally respected and intellectually superior but sexually reserved, would need an alpha female to take the lead. I'm glad I followed my instincts because it was fun and educational for me. This new experience let me realize an aspect of myself that had been hidden. Taking the initiative wasn't even something I myself approved of because I was loyal to the outer authority of patriarchal rule that didn't permit instincts, but rather conformity. This aspect in me had never been let out before. Instead of my habit of pleasing others, I was now pleasing myself and thoroughly enjoying it. Living in the present moment was full of surprises when I let life naturally unfold by listening to my body, heart and mind.

Being in the position of pursuer made me wonder why I would need to wait for a man to make the first move. If I knew I was interested in him, why would I wait? There was a confidence and a natural sensual curiosity in me, that even rejection could not squelch. My Higher Self was not attached. It was not judging, trying, or manipulating. It was observing, sensing and participating with appreciation. I could feel that knowing through the sensations in my body and through my touch. Owning my sensuality was like finding my right arm. It was a natural and comfortable expression of who I am.

When I headed over to The Professor's house, I didn't know I would be asking him to sit in his chair, or that I would ask him to unbuckle his pants, or that I would instruct him to pull out his cock. But that's what happened and I'm not sure if I should be sharing all of those details with you, but it's serving the purpose of helping you to see my process, to better understand your own. I'm not promoting sex with strangers. That is not at all what this is about or what I am interested in. What these experiences offered was a new environment that didn't have a set of rules attached that fixed my beliefs into place. I received the necessary wiggle room to find parts of me. And as a result, I felt a new woman rising up within me after each of my experiences.

I will not apologize for allowing myself to express my sensual desire for The Professor. It was good for both of us. I would guess it was years since he had had a romantic relationship. His mind was content in proving revolutionary theories but his body, at that moment, seemed far more content than ever. He looked younger, lighter, and more alive after his mostly silent orgasm. Only a yelp slipped out during his loss of control. There was no reason for him to try to regain composure so quickly. We've all learned the habit to control life. I personally believe there is a pure innocence of unbridled nature within us and that was something I felt myself tapping into.

I also found myself amazed and curious about the mystery of orgasm. It fascinates me how it puts us in the most vulnerable position. I believe we need to get more comfortable in our vulnerability and realize it's not such a scary place after all. It's actually powerful. It's obvious that we can control our emotions and that both men and women probably do that at the moment of orgasm. But why not ride it out all the way? It's okay to be vulnerable. Our bodies may need that space to reach for more. If you consider the moment of orgasm as a spiritual experience could you let yourself dive into that more?

The Professor hugged me so tight I thought he was going to crush me. He was more the size of a football player than what you may have thought of as a nerdy scientist but it was the nerd in him that attracted me. In these experiences with different men, I learned what attributes I found attractive. When he pulled me against his chest, I could hear his heartbeat in my ear. Feeling his heart and his relaxed breathing against my neck, made me feel like I was holding a tender boy and a very large man at the same

time. It felt good to hold him. I had plenty of heart to do so and I could tell he needed physical touch and was deeply appreciative. It was as if he had forgotten what it felt like to be close and intimate with someone. He whispered in my ear over and over again, "Thank you, thank you, thank you, dear, sweet Andrea, thank you."

Our brief and intimate time together was more than a blip on the radar screen. It was a spike of fresh, new data stored as a feel-good moment in his library of research. For me, it was a part of my living research in my own human understanding. Realized in each new experience and captured as a memory of my own personal growth.

I was learning to follow my instincts, instead of my limited beliefs and old habits. My heart had more space to be open and curious which strengthened my faith and built my trust in it. Each one of those steps brought me new clarity. From that alignment, I was put in new situations that challenged my fears that tried to stop me from reaching for the gold. My Spirit was the gold I was reaching for and that gold could only be found within me. I would have never thought that a closer relationship with my body was how I could better hear my heart. Only in hindsight, in seeing the woman I have become, can I credit these wonderful men for providing me opportunities to face my fears, and transform my limited beliefs and old habits into new realizations of embodiment. My former beliefs, just like yours, are merely thoughts that others taught me to think. I certainly preferred living life through my own choices, and not through the old programs of others.

Chapter 30
The Frenchman

I embraced and faced every one of my unexpected sexual encounters, up until the very last one that followed me onto my flight from France to Brighton, UK. It was a Frenchman who was seated next to me. He was wickedly handsome and very aggressive. I shied away from him and his flirtation being conscientious of the other passengers. He shocked me when he grabbed my face and kissed me, after we sat down next to each other on the plane. My eyes were wide-open.

Although, we were in our own exclusive two-seater side of the plane, and no one would have known we weren't together, I wasn't okay with him grabbing and kissing me. This encounter allowed me to address boundaries and to speak up for myself. I let the Frenchmen know that if he were to try that again I'd have my seat moved. I also made it clear that I prefer the aisle and sitting in the front of the plane, exactly where I was. And those were the only reasons why I didn't get up and ask to be moved. In other words, he would be the one moving if he didn't change his behavior.

Anyone who was once codependent knows that boundary building is hard work. It's not well practiced by most people because we are not taught the importance of boundaries as children. Developing my own bond of affection with myself led me to be more affectionate with others. Boundaries became even more important as a result. In this incident, I was proud of my bravery when I spoke up, and I was happy to hear his apology. He pulled his energy back and gave me space. That felt good.

We spent the rest of the flight chatting as he told me about himself while asking me questions about my life. By the time our flight landed we had a genuine respect for one another. He had apologized for his advances, more than once, and said that there was a strange magnetism he felt that drew him toward me. He said he assumed I felt the same way. I appreciated him expressing that because that unsaid magnetism happened to me more than once in my life and it wasn't mutual. Although, men believed it was.

It was good to hear him articulate what was happening on his end for me to get a better sense of what others had experienced with me. That is why consensual is so important, it eliminates assumptions and it puts both parties in a position of power. Mutual respect wins in open communication. We might not like what the other person says when they are honest but it's important to learn. Since we are moving toward shared power, where no one is dominate over another, it's good to practice the opposite of self-censoring. It opens up communication and bonding.

We exited the plane together and stopped near the bathrooms to say goodbye. He asked if he could hug me. I thanked him for asking first and said, "Yes!" Our warm embrace was interrupted by a mother trying to come out of the family bathroom behind us. We both apologized and stepped aside. He grabbed the door to hold it open for her and her child to exit. Once they made it out, a busy traveler rushing by assumed he was holding the door for me, and abruptly barked, "Go ahead!" I giggled to myself and walked in. The Frenchman followed me. We turned and locked the door. Since this is the end of my sexual share, I'll leave this last encounter to your imagination. Even if it was just a French kiss, it was the first one I ever had with a Frenchman.

Conclusion of Part II

My travels were an unimagined fantasy come to life. They were experiences that helped me face my beliefs and limitations around my body and the shame of sex. I didn't foresee a Frenchman or any of the lovers who showed up on my journey abroad. Other than expecting to be with Jesus, that was still its own surprise at Aphrodite's Rock. It took a lot of bravery on my part to face the demons of judgment that arose in my mind and body when I allowed myself to receive affection and pleasure. Believe it or not I was engaging with the things that frightened me because I had learned at such a young age that my body was bad, and that it was controlled by someone outside of me.

I was taught that sex wasn't about my pleasure because religion and one sex education video in sixth grade was all the education I ever received. Other than my mother having me put on birth control when I began menstruating, and there still was no conversation about sex. What a huge disservice to me and to all females who have been put in a similar position. That is what shame and lack of information does. It paints us into corners until we face what we have been conditioned to be frightened of.

I came to discover my creativity, compassion, joy, and a love for myself in heart mind and body through these, and more experiences that came to me. I realized that I deserved to be honored and that it was my responsibility to honor me first. In that honoring, I came to see the currency in the bonds I formed with men had mutual like and respect. My integrity was sourced in my body and how it felt in that moment. From that place of connection, I offered honesty and emotional expression that came from a place of pure love. There weren't expectations or preconceived notions attached in the spontaneity of what arose.

Like you, I had built a strong mental body that knew how to think through things, but these encounters challenged me to get more into my body. From that place, I was more freely giving to myself and others. It became about doing what the integrity of me felt moved to do, in that moment, depending on my body which didn't have an agenda like my mind did. The act of receiving and giving affection was fulfilling. It changed me as a woman. My old habits of living strictly in my mental body didn't teach me that pleasure, affection and happiness were mine to have. Or that my heart communication was experienced through my body.

My muscle of awareness grew through personal life experiences and helped me to see that I wasn't a victim of the old programs and patterns designed by others. When I caught sight of them with my awareness - I then had choice. The integrity of me came from my body in the moment as a wiser council than my prior learned habits and beliefs.

I'm not promoting random acts of sex with strangers, or trying to get you all hot and horny to stroke one off. I am showing you a part of my human evolution that had me face tough fears to move beyond them. The women reading this section will relate more to my internal experience than the men because we are indoctrinated to turn against our own bodies. These sexual experiences taught me so much about the woman I am, what I enjoy, what is possible, how much there is to love and appreciate about a man. And, how comfortable I am in my sensual skin. If man didn't determine my thoughts but a natural order designed as my body did, I could live in a freedom of expression by listening, in each moment to the integrity of my body and do what I felt moved to do. That came from a place of giving, not from a program of survival.

How in the world I gave myself permission to explore, travel, and feel pleasure is beyond me. I credit my Highest Self for leading the voyage that brought me adventures, new perspectives, and flavors of life I didn't even know existed. Becoming aware of my physical, emotional, mental, and spiritual body was a process. Daily, I still integrate my limitless nature as I choose to believe in my highest and greatest potential. Not knowing the form it will take but feeling a more natural order take form in my own life that just feels right.

By no means, do I discredit the mental body, which is an important component in life. But without the physical and emotional, which naturally produces the spiritual, my high-performance vehicle (and an orgasm) didn't exist for me. As all four aspects became more integrated as a whole; my life became far more satisfying, natural and interesting.

I appreciate the loyalty and closeness of a committed romantic relationship. However, the particular beliefs and fears I needed to overcome around my body, only came as a result of sampling life outside the box of normalcy. It took courage to live outside the traditional expectations of society and engage with the things that frightened me. But as a result, touching, tasting, communicating, and connecting with different men was an education beyond any book I could have ever read. Twenty years of schooling didn't teach me what I learned through personal experience.

My appreciation and curiosity about men blossomed to the point where I am now in service to men all around the world. I am a champion for their feelings and respect their mental capabilities. My currency of emotional expression and life knowledge continue to bring solid bonds into my life; both professionally and personally. My natural honoring of women is why the velvety layer of this book is dedicated to them. I magnetize a strong male clientele but that does not mean I do not work with strong women too.

My travels opened me up to people, places, mysteries, pleasures and new perspectives. Fear no longer needed to control me but could teach me who I was when I braved the "unknown." I was rewarded with more love each time I used my curiosity and courage to go into my fears and tough emotions, and free myself. The wisdom could only be found on the other side of the old belief, habit and thought. To know myself, I needed to know who I was not. Which was a huge identity crisis. I truly believed I was shy and lived the role as a codependent, submissive woman. It was shocking to discover how comfortable I was in my independence, and to meet the huntress in me who goes for what she wants. Underneath the lies I lived as truth - I found my sensual, affectionate nature as natural as nature herself.

Being in the realization, knowing and physical embodiment of my true nature, I do not consent to religion, society or any organization controlling a pure, powerful and natural part of who

I am. I do not need anyone's permission to become all that I can be, other than my own. I am a sovereign being who is confident in who I am, and in the roles that I serve to inspire millions to know thyself. For me, that took stripping layers of conditioning and bad habits. By being willing to take an honest look at myself I made room for my heart which speaks to me through my body.

No one outside of me gets to decide who I am anymore. I have become a teacher and a source of inspiration to great leaders, business owners and people of all ages. I offer my authenticity and warm heart to welcome you home - to yours. I fell into the bunker, I burnt my steak, and I rose up and out of the traps of life, to touch you with my juicy, affectionate awareness.

I hope my intimate encounters have inspired you to rise with me, in becoming awake and aware in our world today. As you can see healing my thoughts (mind) and feelings (heart) was extremely important to healing my body. And it is why I will continually remind you that **healing is to be respected**. When it is, mankind will no longer feed the separation that has existed between the heart and the mind. Or the male and the female. We move from separation into a connectedness with our own heart and one another. I chose to become the solution and so can you.

Sex & Balances to Come

After I returned from my travels abroad, I moved to California before the year ended. I began my master's program in late January. The years between then and now continued to shape me as I returned to committed relationships redefining what worked for me. I have learned so much that I can't wait to share more with you.

This was going to be the start of Part III but you've earned yourself a break. I promise to engage your thinking from the start of my next book. It begins with the big O. I summarize important facts about the female body for both the men and the ladies to read in the chapter that follows. I'm sure you'll enjoy the whole Sex & Balances section.

Like one piece of clothing being ripped off after the next, one realization at a time began to strip me naked of the old images and identities that once defined me. Once I became conscious of what was unconscious, I had the power of choice over those areas of my life; an awareness of my free-will. My life became "a progressive realization of a worthy ideal" which is another way of saying - I became successful on my own terms. That is still taking form in my life as My Higher Kingdom becomes its own Academy in the realms of spirit and science.

My new relationship with my body was a way for me to hear my heart through my own flesh. When I aligned with the wisdom in me; I embraced traits and characteristics of a playful, sensual, curious, soft, open, strong, and wise me. I learned to embrace and ride the force within me. I moved from a dense, 'I want to get it right' linear reality, to a 'I trust and allow' heart-aligned magnetism. That is the place of expansion and where I continue to travel.

In that 'cookie jar quantum field of knowing' within me, that feels like nature herself, I want to explore more of my own human potential. That will be exciting because each of you will get to come along for the ride. I am inviting you to join me. Until you embrace more of your own limitlessness, my wildly alive nature will tease you in.

Tesla spoke about the importance of the non-physical phenomena of who we are - as being the most useful study that science refuses to accept. I am my own researcher and scientific study and I will boldly say, "Just because science refuses to accept the whole of what makes us human, that doesn't mean we should too!"

Each of us contributes to the whole with our thoughts and actions. If we could see our own frequency, we would realize our impact. That is why I am asking you to sense that which cannot be seen. I inspire you to get more in touch with your own body. Develop a mastery where you feel the subtleties of your frequency. Adopt habits that expand your bandwidth. You know what brings you down and what brings you up. Discovering my unconscious thoughts and beliefs that were turning my dial down, gave me the power to adjust it upward.

That's a responsibility worth taking seriously. Now that you know the most powerful technology in the universe is within you, why not put it to good use? My seduction is about a platter of power that I hold up - for you to see you. I inspire more of your greatness to come forth in your own personal life and in the work that you do. That is the power that redefines what's come before.

After stripping my old beliefs, I stepped into my tailored made Higher Self that was waiting for me all along. I'm still in the glorious process of going from ordinary to extraordinary. My exploration of my limitless nature continues to this day. I invite you to be a part of my next book by corresponding with me to share what you have learned about you. Summarize it in a paragraph and up to one page.

As a researcher of my own inner phenomenon and limitless potential, I will continue to share what I discover in subsequent books. You already know how the next book will start. If you would like me to include examples of other people's discoveries, share your own with me. Tell me how you sense the connection to your heart and how you've deepened it. My continued work will include hosting open dialogs that will expose questions from my readers and those in attendance. Join me on my podcast until our society opens up and into a larger freedom of expression.

I know who I am. My freedom is powerful and it's contagious. You can trust that my voice will continue to express my individual thoughts, feelings, ideas and experiences as a teacher of the seen and unseen. I am grateful to be a forerunner in what's to come, and to have you join me as co-creators of a life we live with heart.

There is so much more for me to uncover. This is just the beginning of My Higher Kingdom here on earth. In my next book, I will continue to push the envelope to provoke new possibilities. In the light of what I see that is now coming to an end, I welcome you to open up to your: limitless potential, natural healing abilities, real wealth, happiness and freedom of creativity. As you now see - I am here to stir things up a bit; on behalf of the highest and greatest good of all. You probably didn't realize that blowing your mind could be such a good thing. Get ready for more when you delve into the first chapter of my next book, "The Hidden Power of Orgasm." The first page will be wet and ready for you. If you so dare... please join me.

"Conscious awareness of existence - is life." ~*Andrea Elliott*

Unit We Meet Again

Until we meet again, may you move through your life with my affection (and your own) felt: in your deep breath, the sunrise, a sunset, a hot bath, a walk through the forest, the breeze across your skin, a dip in the ocean, and in every moment that you are present. Imagine me cheering your bravery when you align with your highest and greatest potential. **Your heart is valuable. Our future depends on your investment in it**.

Please Stay in Touch

Find me at: http://www.myhigherkingdom.podbean.com or find me on Apple Podcasts and iHeart Radio. You can also find me on Instagram and at www.MyHigherKingdom.com . Let me know what inspired you. What you are learning about your own feelings, body wisdom and source connection by emailing me myhigherkingdom@gmail.com I welcome your participation in my next book by remaining anonymous. Gender, age, and city or country of residence, along with a made-up nickname is all that we need to include with your human understanding.

Share your perspectives or questions about feelings, how you connect with your heart or sexual quandaries that are typically left unsaid. We are in the process of redefining the new human. The more knowledge we share - the better. **Warning:** No pornography or hateful remarks welcomed. My energy is not intended for narcissists, socio-paths or beings void of Spirit. I said it before, and I'm saying it again. My audience is of the light.

Thank you for spending this time with me my strong, sweet, cuddly, handsome lions, and curious, courageous women. A big, passionate hug to you all. I value and appreciate your loving hearts and your eager bodies that seek your attention and affection. I cherish your presence and your growing awareness. You matter! We need you!

I am one woman sharing my thoughts, feelings, experiences, and perspectives with you. They may create new possibilities and healing opportunities in your life but **it is you who is the authority over you.**

Thank you again for joining me in My Higher Kingdom. I hope to hear you roar for me sometime soon. In the meantime, I am sensually touching you with my words and eternally calling you home - into your heart.

Until we meet again, between the pages of my next book, join me on my podcast to hear my words live. I appreciate you sharing my book with those who would benefit. Please keep on dreaming, changing and building your muscle of awareness - to flex for me when I see you next.

All my love and respect,
Andrea

Bibliography

Books:

Ware. B. (2017) *Top Five Regrets of the Dying*. Bolinda Publishing Pty. Ltd.

Yogananda, P (1950) *Autobiography of a Yogi*. Los Angeles, CA: Self Realization Fellowship

Internet:

Dotson S. (2015, October 17). *Wilhelm Reich Orgone Energy Documentary*. From Floating Lodge YouTube Channel   https://youtu.be/BKiK5afXYgg

Hobbs, J. https://www.oraclegirl.org

Lipton, B. https://www.brucelipton.com/

Acknowledgments

Thank you for your presence. This book is for you, and us. It's for our wildly alive hearts that radiate our new human potential into existence. It's for the nature that lives in us, and as us.

Thank you to all the men who opened their hearts, minds and bodies to me, in my life and through these pages. Thank you to each one of you who march with me. I respect your courage to claim what is rightfully yours.

I give thanks to the women who have stood by me through my continuous change, and to those who were there at the start. Thank you to all the women who support other women in being all that they can be.

I give thanks to our beautiful planet that abundantly provides for us all. I acknowledge nature wholeheartedly.

A big thank you in advance to our highest and greatest good being supported and realized in the hearts of humanity. The endless peace and beauty I perceive as the new life we create together is of the highest splendor.

I toast to us, and our good fortune of living in alignment. We shall reap the rich rewards of creating from a place where we know - we have everything we need before we even begin. Here's to us!